# DEATH, THE DEVIL
# AND TAM O'SHANTER

# DEATH, THE DEVIL AND TAM O'SHANTER

*The Supernatural World of Robert Burns*

Written & Illustrated by
Tom Douglas

The Book Guild Ltd
Sussex, England

First published in Great Britain in 2002 by
The Book Guild Ltd
25 High Street
Lewes, East Sussex
BN7 2LU

Typesetting in Times by
Acorn Bookwork, Salisbury, Wiltshire

Printed in Great Britain by
Bookcraft (Bath) Ltd, Avon

A catalogue record for this book is available from
The British Library.

ISBN 1 85776 661 X

*To Shirley, as ever, though she can no longer see clearly the images I create*

*Alice was beginning to get very tired of sitting by her sister on the bank, and of having nothing to do; once or twice she had peeped into the book her sister was reading, but it had no pictures or conversations in it 'and what is the use of a book,' thought Alice, 'without pictures or conversations?'*

Lewis Carroll

# CONTENTS

# LIST OF ILLUSTRATIONS

PROLOGUE

In one sense it seems an entirely unnecessary exercise to present some of the work of Robert Burns to a general public which has had access to it for over 200 years. Much has been written about the works and Burns's life has been covered in minute detail both by contemporaries and by later writers exploring various aspects of his short life of 37 years. Yet from another point of view each generation comes to Robert Burns's work from a different angle and can see things in his work which were to his contemporaries commonplace, but which to later generations appear strange and in need of some explanation. There is some danger that in this process the poems will tend to be taken at their face value, the songs, the love poems, the letters, the satires will be taken out of the social context in which they were written. Alternatively, for those more sociologically inclined their value will reside in the insights they can offer about the society in which Burns lived. Either of these approaches is essentially valid and may well fulfil what different individuals can gain from reading the works of Burns. I have always, from first reading 'Tam o'Shanter', been intrigued not so much by a rollicking story beautifully and concisely told, as by the use Burns made of creatures of the supernatural.

Why did a farmer's son, almost entirely self-educated, whose intellect was admittedly only limited by the books he was able to access, write four poems where the supernatural was an essential ingredient? The simplest answer is of course that in them Burns was writing poetry not just to be printed in books and read around firesides, but he was using his skill as a poet to impress ideas upon people, to illustrate common behaviour, prejudices and wrongs. In order to do this he needed, as all efficient communicators do, a language that was familiar to the people he wanted to reach, one where the meanings attached to words would be held in common by all his hearers and readers and he needed to use ideas and feelings, superstitions and beliefs, traditions and customs that were also common.

He lived in a society which at one end had urban intellectuals devoted to the pursuit of reason and rational understanding and at the other a large agricultural population largely dominated by the Calvinist church, whose lives were hard and practical and for whom tradition and usage largely dictated the daily patterns of their existence to a very great extent.

The four poems which I have presented here all had specific targets in those populations and all used some aspect of the supernatural as part of the approach. Burns was not the first poet to write of holding a discourse with Death but he was unique in the purpose for which this discourse was recounted. Nor was he the first by a long way to record an appeal to the Devil to diminish his harassment of lowly mortals. His poem 'Halloween' has a different target in that whether for his own instruction or that of others he was recording the traditional practices of country folk and how, though the element of terror at the possibility of the actual existence of supernatural beings was still there, these practices had become suffused with some half-hearted disbelief in the reality of such creatures and overlaid with an element of fun still made sharp by a residual instinctive awe. 'Tam o'Shanter' – which Burns regarded as his best work – is rather more complex in that it postulates retribution for those, who, through insobriety, blunder into the world of the supernatural. But perhaps more importantly it foregrounds the essentially masculine lack of consideration for others which Burns clearly saw existed in his society and from which he himself was not exactly immune.

That society, or that part of it which was not urban, was very prone to ascribe the causes of unexpected events to agents whose powers exceeded the known powers of the laws of nature. They tended to believe that an unknown and mysterious spiritual force existed everywhere and was oftimes made manifest by unusual and inexplicable events, by the appearance of and interference of occult beings. Burns had every reason not only to know about these beliefs but also to have experienced the effects they produced. He was a rational man, but he lived in a social context where the occult had made a strong impression on him as a child, and despite the application of his intelligence he was aware of a different kind of knowing about such things which had no basis in reason.

Why illustrate the poems?

Well, in a sense to illustrate the characters and creatures that Burns wrote about in his poems is to continue into another medium the process that he himself started. His verbal description of the Devil on two occasions and of Death on another are embodiments in words of the fearful imaginings of the people of the lowland countryside. What I have attempted to do is to embody those characters and creatures in visual images which are in keeping, not with modern phantasies of the unknown, but in the human-like forms with which Burns's contemporaries would have endowed them. Thus Death is skeletal with a thin covering of skin tufted with hair and sporting a beard, the Devil is sooty dark and his minions torturers, in various semi-human guises, of terrified humans. In 'Tam o'Shanter' I have used distortions of the human form for the witches who were after all human beings who had not been changed from their original shape when they made a pact with the Devil who is shown in Alloway's old kirk as a black dog.

We live in a society which is increasingly beset by images to some detriment of the power of the word so, it is with this in mind that I have provided visual images to accompany Burns's extremely powerful and far superior verbal creations. As far as I am aware the first illustrations of Burns's work were made for 'Tam o' Shanter' by David Allan, an almost exact contemporary of the poet. Behind all this lies the mocking humour which could be savage when it was directed at what Burns saw as injustice or harmful prejudice, gentle when he wished it to be so as in his sympathy for the Devil, taunting when he describes his fellow mason and school teacher as Dr Hornbook, implying that the dominie was a charlatan. But there is in all of the poems presented here a sense that Burns was laughing, often quite gently, not only at those he portrays in his poems, but at his hearers and readers as well. There is frequently a strong hint also that his laughter included himself as a target as when he inevitably portrays himself as being somewhat less than sober when he encounters these supernatural creatures.

The brief biographical comments are not intended to add up to a 'life' of the poet but merely to indicate the current state of his social existence at the time of writing the poems discussed here. Essentially these snippets of his life are employed to demonstrate, where they are known, the emotional states of the poet and the triggers which precipitated his writing. As I have noted, all four poems mentioned were targetted at specific people or written for specific purposes which, with the possible exception of the 'Address to the Devil', derived from events or persons other than the poet himself. The chronology of Burns's life is given primarily to place the events of the years of the poems in the context of his life as a whole, dreadfully short as it was.

It is necessary, I think, to resolve how many poems are actually used here. In fact three are given in full, that is 'Death and Dr Hornbook', 'The Address to the Devil' and, of course, 'Tam o'Shanter'. 'Halloween', which also has a supernatural basis is referred to but the text is not given in full for two very simple reasons. Whereas the lowland Scots vernacular which Burns uses in the other three poems is easily intelligible to the English reader, the language of 'Halloween' is not. Burns when he wrote this poem was using a vocabulary which was all but obsolete in 1785. The second reason is that it is a long poem because it is essentially a catalogue of the traditional country practices of All Hallows Eve, which, while very interesting as a record of eighteenth-century lowland Scots behaviour, contains far less material on supernatural beings and infinitely more about the transactions human beings attempt to make with them.

Finally a word about the description of these works of Burns as 'diablerie' by contemporary commentators. Essentially the word implies the practice of sorcery or devilry, that is magic or witchcraft connected with devils. But it is also used to refer to the practice of mischief and in this latter sense is very applicable to Burns's essays into the supernatural. However, there is yet a third meaning ascribed to 'diablerie' which implies an esoteric knowledge of devils which, used by Burns commentators might have meant that they thought he appeared to possess knowledge of such creatures beyond the common level. As we shall see, Burns was inducted into quite a vast repertoire of knowledge about supernatural beings in his childhood, but the repository of this knowledge and the one who imparted it to the poet was an old female relative who had a lifetime's experience of hearing and remembering the stories of her associates, which, in the final assessment, can hardly be called esoteric however extensive they were.

It is not intended that this book should be seen as a serious in-depth analysis of one aspect of Burns's poetic works. That would indeed be presumptuous in the extreme for several simple reasons. Supernatural imagery occurred in a very small proportion of Burns's output so any intensive analysis would be disproportionate to that output. But perhaps more importantly from the view of the twenty first century Burns was only making the unreal appear 'real', creating a virtual reality for his audience when it suited his purpose. He knew that anthropomorphic creations of the concepts of death and evil were already widely available to his audience. And thirdly he wrote with humour about such things and with a lightness of touch which belied his own deep understanding both experiential and philosophical of the human condition that a 'heavy' investigation of his means would be out of place.

# 1

# THE SUPERNATURAL WORLD OF ROBERT BURNS

Robert Burns (1759/96) in his short life produced a considerable body of poems, epistles, satires and songs covering most aspects of life in lowland Scotland in the late eighteenth century. He was not unduly preoccupied with supernatural beings and only once with Death as an apparition, though Death as a fact of life was mentioned in a good many of his works especially in epitaphs of his friends.

Indeed only four of his works, 'Death and Dr Hornbook', the 'Address to the Devil', 'Halloween' and 'Tam o'Shanter' are expressly concerned with the supernatural and all are informed with Burns's notable sense of humour. In the case of 'Dr Hornbook', Burns hit on the idea of personalising the devil and of holding conversation with him as a means of expressing his concern about the quack medical practices of the schoolmaster at Tarbolton. As is usual with Burns he casts himself in a state of semi-drunkenness as the individual to whom the Devil appears to make a case against the schoolmaster for curing those whom the devil would kill and for killing those in whom the devil has no interest.

The interesting description of the devil in this poem bears a striking resemblance to those 'Deaths' of a decidedly skeletal nature which had appeared for hundreds of years before Burns's time in the illustration of books by artists like Holbein and Hollar (see Illustration from Holbein's *Dance of Death*). Though Burns quite significantly reduces the terrifying aspect of such a figure to the point where the devil complains that he has become a target of the mockery of small children in the village of Tarbolton who poke the finger of scorn at him and pull the tufts of hair which adorn his body. Yet he is still

3

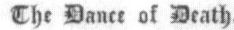

The Dance of Death.

No. XLIII—THE KNIGHT OR SOLDIER.

When a strong man armed keepeth his palace, his goods are in peace; but when a stronger than he shall come upon him, and overcome him, he taketh from him all his armour wherein he trusted, and divideth his spoils.----*Luke*, xi. 21, 22.

UNDAUNTED and secure in arms,
While strength and life remain,
The brave his mansions, and his wealth,
In safety dares maintain.

But Death with greater force shall wage
Against him war ere long,
And for the grave shall make him quit
His post, however strong.

G 2

No. XLII. THE KNIGHT OR SOLDIER.
When a strong man armed keepeth his palace, his goods are in peace; but when a stronger than he shall come upon him, and overcome him, he taketh from him all his armour wherein he trusted, and divideth his spoils.
Luke.xi.21,22.

4

skeletal in form with 'fient a wame', no belly to speak of, but his bones are barely covered with skin and the aforementioned tufts of hair. He wears a beard and carries a three-pronged spear and of course the ubiquitous scythe.

When Burns came to write 'Tam o'Shanter' he had once again recourse to the idea that before supernatural manifestations could emerge in tangible form the person who saw them was necessarily in a well-liquored state. Where he is describing the activities of supernatural beings as in his 'Address to the Devil', there is no suggestion of intoxication and consequently imaginative delineation takes the place of described actual manifestation.

In the *Monthly Review* of December 1786, the comments on the Kilmarnock edition of Burns's poetry, included the following on 'Halloween':

> ... particularly 'Halloween', which contains a lively picture of the magical tricks that are still practised in the country at that season. It is a valuable relic which, like Vergil's eighth eclogue, will preserve the memory of these simple incantations long after they would otherwise have been lost.

Robert Heron in his *Memoirs of the Life of Robert Burns* dated 1797, discussed Burns's ability to depict the common rural life and had this to say about 'Halloween':

> A thousand prejudices of Popish, and perhaps too of ruder Pagan superstition, have from time immemorial; been connected in the minds of the Scottish peasantry, with the annual occurrence of the Eve of the Festival of all the Saints, or Hallowe'en. These were all intimately known to Burns, and had made a powerful impression upon his imagination and feelings. Choosing them for the subject of a poem, he produced a piece, which is, almost to a frenzy, the delight of those who are best acquainted with the subject; and which will not fail to preserve the memory of the prejudices and usages which it describes,

when they shall, perhaps, have ceased to give one merry evening in the year to the cottage fireside.

In 'Halloween' indeed Burns describes in great detail not so much the appearance of or imagined activities of supernatural beings as the behaviour of country folk in respect of traditional practices of prophesy, divination etc. which, although they imply the presence and action of such beings and awe and indeed fear are involved, do not require manifestation or presence. For this reason although reference will be made to 'Halloween' it is not quoted in full here.

Burns also notes that much of the origins of these practices has been lost over time and that what is left consists mainly of routines and traditional behaviours which, while still being significantly frightening enough to be exciting are also regarded as a means to quite ordinary ends e.g. of courting and are thus consonant with being regarded with some sense of fun. In both 'Dr Hornbook' and the 'Address to the Devil' Burns's own sense of humour, while quite marked as usual, is overlaid by an unmistakable feeling of pity for both the supernatural manifestations he has conjured up. In the case of Death it is a necessary tactic and part of his objective in exposing the schoolmaster that his poem should evoke some sympathy for Death in what, in modern times, would be called a 'demarcation dispute'. If even Death has had to complain about his practices being usurped, Burns is saying then there is something markedly wrong with the behaviour of Death's competitor!

Burns's exposure of the schoolmaster's practices has often been assumed to have had the desired result and their perpetrator fled to Glasgow and eventually obtained a secure job there and is on record as being somewhat grateful to the poet for having been the means of forcing him into it. It is something of a pity that Burns did not have time in his short life to write another poem of a second meeting with Death in which the latter could have expressed his thanks for the removal of his rival.

The 'Address to the Devil' is a different matter. In the first instance the poem is basically a request to the devil to reduce his persecution of mankind. A short list of these inflicted hurts is included which contains reference to individuals being smitten with ailments and the respite being requested is personal as well as general. There is some hint towards the end of the poem that the devil may be inclined to dismiss the request on the grounds that the poet would have to be drunk to make it. But Burns suggests that he is not drunk and indeed expresses some pity for the devil whose role is so wholly concerned to torment humans without mercy.

Here the devil is not made manifest but he is described as flying over moors and hills in the company of warlocks and witches, of being able to pry into human souls and his appearance is suggested by reference to fellow poets, so that we see that Burns is using the church's traditional depiction of Satan and those of early writers in the subject, the devil is black, horned, winged and of evil countenance. It is interesting that although Burns was familiar with descriptions of the devil as he was originally held to be i.e. as an archangel, a splendid prince of heaven before his expulsion, that he had also read Milton's *Paradise Lost* as witness his reference to the Archangel Michael cutting Satan with his sword in the battle between the forces of Good and Evil, he chooses to use an image of the devil which would have been much more familiar to the ordinary people of his time. Thus the devil is black or sooty, winged and in all respects similar to the paintings which had been on the walls of churches from the Saxon period onwards, a description which would have been in every-day use by the Calvinist preachers of the period who were by and large firmly convinced of the existence of the devil as affirmed by the scriptures. Burns's iconography and images are simple and direct, designed to be familiar to his expected audiences. For instance it was commonly held that the devil present during a witches' sabbath usually assumed a form other than that of a human being like the great Goat of Mendes or as Burns presented him in 'Tam o'Shanter' as a large shaggy dog.

When Burns came to write 'Tam o'Shanter' it is plain that

his mind and his memory were already well stocked with the images he would need. He was surrounded by a farming community which still had strong superstitions and fears, an even stronger Calvinist church where the power of the devil was openly preached as a threat to humankind and supernatural beings directly invoked. The laws against witchcraft had only recently been withdrawn and the Catholic church's pronouncements against such practices had been long enduring and powerful which had served to create a substantial belief in people that such a condemnation must mean the actual reality of what was condemned. Thus witchcraft and devil worship had maintained a powerful grip on the popular imagination and with the help of the poetic inspiration that he was able to draw from Milton and other poets, the images of painters and the traditional folklore of his countrymen, Burns was well equipped to make a great impact.

'Tam o'Shanter' is a story – indeed it is the only truly narrative poem that Burns ever published though it is possible that he created drafts for others which he never used and this will be discussed later.

In the four poems considered here Burns gives us a humorous, sympathetic portrait of the beliefs and practices of the country folk of Lowland Scotland in the late eighteenth century which contrasts quite markedly and with great clarity the growing rationalism of the cities and of the intelligentsia of the period. Without Burns and others like Hogg this area of human belief may well never have been so well illuminated – that he did the same for other more general aspects of existence is obviously true. But it required a man of Burns's intellectual satire, humour and perception and sympathy and indeed courage to use what was known as 'diablerie' to make satirical comment, to amuse, instruct and entertain.

## Early Influences

Robert Burns was born into that period of history known as the 'Age of Enlightenment', when rational thought was believed by the intelligentsia to hold the answer to all social and moral problems. He died in the so-called 'Age of Revolution', when the old order of society was being increasingly challenged, notably in France. Indeed, Burns, in the early part of his adult life, was a fervent believer in the republican cause and having taught himself the French language in his youth, he was perhaps better able to appreciate how the aims of the revolution matched his own ideas about his own society.

For most ordinary people the big changes in thinking and politics and religion had little impact except in so far as conflict in the Kirk between traditionalists and more liberal thinkers took place before their eyes. Folklore, superstition and in particular a still powerful belief in supernatural beings and of the power of some of their fellows to affect the quality of life of others seriously was still rife. Spells, divination, charms, prophecy and the terrors of the evil incantation, were an everyday part of their existence, but most often revealed on special occasions like Halloween. This may have been the period of Mozart, William Blake, Galvans, Bentham and Washington but the legacy of superstitions which had existed since pagan times was still strong and would in fact, as we now know, never entirely disappear.

Some indications of the conflicts and beliefs of eighteenth-century Scotland is revealed in the behaviour of the Church.

Scotland was very strongly Calvinist and nowhere more so than in the villages and the country areas. The Church had a great hold over the behaviour of its members. For example it believed that those who had committed the sin of fornication should be required to subject themselves to public penance. This usually comprised of the 'culprit' so designated, usually without more proof than rumour, gossip or report, standing on a stool in the front of the Church for three Sundays in a row, while there they were subjected to a sermon preached explicitly at them and their behaviour. It is known that Burns was himself committed in this manner on several occasions.

Indeed, Burns's first poem which was made public was written in protest at this kind of commitment which had been inflicted upon his friend Gavin Hamilton. Technically Hamilton was 'prosecuted' by the Kirk session for his neglect of the Sabbath, practically what was involved was that he employed a poor man to harvest the potato crop out of his garden on a Sunday.

The charges against Hamilton were brought by the Reverend W. Auld, commonly known as 'Daddy' Auld, and were four in number:

1. Absences from church.
2. Journeying to Carrick on the Sabbath.
3. Neglect of family worship.
4. Having written an abusive letter to Session.

Auld prosecuted Hamilton first at the Presbytery of Ayr on 25th June 1785 and later at the Synod of Glasgow and Ayr, in both instances the verdict went against him and for Hamilton. He was defended by a Robert Aikin, a writer, who lived in Ayr, and who later became a friend of Burns. The poem in question was 'The Twa Herds' and referred to the boundary dispute which had occurred between Moodie a minster of Riccarton and Russell an assistant minister of Kilmarnock. Both men belonged to a Church party called 'The Auld Licht', technically High Calvinists, a stern group who held to the doctrine that only those elected by God were to be saved, all others were for ever damned. Also they believed in original sin and the literal truth of a brimstone hell.

They were opposed in most matters by another Church party who were known as followers of the 'New Licht', a more rational and liberal party with softer views on divine justice and goodness. Gavin Hamilton was a member of this latter party.

With such power over the minds of Kirk members, such a horror as a doctrine of irrevocable destiny, there is no doubt that the existence of the devil and his followers were a potent force in the daily lives of country folk. So it is no surprise to find that a strong belief in witchcraft, devils etc. still retained much of its power.

Certain dates fix the end of Scottish witchcraft. On May 3, 1709 Elspeth Ross was the last person tried before the Court of Judiciary on a general charge of being a notorious witch and of making threats. She was branded and banished. In June 1727 Janet Horne was burned at Dornoch, Ross-shire, for having used her daughter as a flying-horse, the devil shoeing her so that she was permanently lamed. The Judge, Captain David Ross, dismissed charges against the daughter, however. In June 1736, the 'Acts anentes – Witchcraft' was formally repealed. Almost forty years later (1773) the Divines of the Associated Presbytery passed a resolution declaring their belief in witchcraft – just one more indicator of the part the ministers played in encouraging superstition. In 1938 George F. Black was able to give names to 1800 Scottish witches, not all of whom were executed – but he had calculated that over all some 4400 witches had been burned.

R. H. Robbins (1964: 45)

Most of the clergy took as the text of their condemnation of witchcraft and also as proof of its existence Exodus XXII.18, where it is written, 'Thou shalt not suffer a witch to live.' Modern scholars of the Hebrew texts, however, point out the error of this stance because the Hebrew word *Kaskagh* taken to mean 'witch' in actual fact is more literally translated as 'poisoner'.

When the associated Presbytery made their declaration of belief in witchcraft, Robert Burns was 14 years old.

Although strong attempts had been made by the Catholic Church to eradicate witchcraft from the time of Pope Alexander IV who, in 1258 had ordered the Inquisition to deal with it particularly if linked with heresy; to Innocent VII's *Summis Desiderantes Affectibus* of (1484). (That is 'Desiring with most profound anxiety'). This, according to Robbins, '... fastened on European jurisprudence for nearly three centuries the duty of combatting the devil and saving mankind from his clutches ... it served as justification for pitiless persecution' (p. 263).

Witchcraft was made a felony in England in 1542, an act which led to the persecution of countless old women resulting in many deaths and witchcraft became a capital offence in 1563 and subject to a death sentence in Scotland the same year.

Witch-finders like Matthew Hopkins had operated through the 1640s and throughout the seventeenth century the Presbyterians pursued alleged witches with great vigour. The important points of this animadversion into the history of witchcraft are two: firstly the belief in their actual existence had been extremely strong as marked by the long continuing use of force, law and condemnation against them; and secondly that the last trial for witchcraft in England took place in 1712, and in Scotland in 1722 only 34 years before Robert Burns was born. Indeed the laws on the statute books of England and Scotland were only repealed in 1736.

What Burns has Tam o'Shanter encounter in the poem is a witches' Sabbath. According to traditional beliefs these took place at midnight involving witches, demons etc. It was also believed by some to have been an annual event, but other authorities suggest that four dates were used particularly by cult members in the Middle Ages. These were Candlemas, the second of February, the churches' celebration of the Feast of the Purification of the Virgin; Lammas, on the first of August; the old harvest festival known as at the Loaf Mass; Roodmass on the fourteenth of September; Holyrood Day, and the most frequent date, the thirty-first of October, All Hallows Eve – Halloween. Celebrations lasted until dawn and the rites were performed by a group of 12 witches known as the coven and one devil. There is no date given in Burns's poem for the Sabbath that Tam witnessed, but the weather was cold and stormy and Burns had showed interest otherwhere in the functions of Halloween, so perhaps the thirty-first of October would be the most likely date to assume.

Burns showed some quite considerable interest in 'diablerie' as it can be discovered in several of his poems notably in his 'Address to the De'il' written in 1785, that is five years before 'Tam o'Shanter'. In it Burns shows his knowledge of the beliefs of the country dwellers of his area. It is hard to believe that such an intelligent and insightful person as the poet demonstrably was could have believed in a personal devil. But he does put across a feeling that he is half-minded to ascribe a lot of the trials of mankind at least to some supernatural and malevolent agency. Yet in a letter of 10th September 1792 to Alexander Cunningham, a lawyer whom he had met in Edinburgh, Burns wrote:

'... you must know, I have set a nipperkin of Toddy by me, just by way of a Spell, to keep away the meikle horned De'il, or any of his subaltern Imps who may be on their nightly rounds.' He goes on in the letter to write of 'Spirit, Bogles, Brownie, with an iron flail, kelpie haunting the ford or ferry; Ghost making nocturnal visits, performing mistic rights, standing by the bedside of the Villain or the Murderer.' He admits that these things help him to write and he says, 'I feel, I feel, the presence of Supernatural assistance!'

In verses 9–13 of his 'Address to the De'il' Burns writes of

13

the creatures of superstition which, from various sources, we know he had learned of as a child from Betty Davidson:

Let warlocks grim, an' wither'd hags,
Tell how wi' you, on ragweed nags'
They skim the muirs an dizzy crags'
        Wi' wicked speed,
And in kirk-yards renew their leagues
        Owre howket dead.

Thence countra wives wi' toil an' pain,
May plunge an' plunge the kirn in vain;
For oh! The yellow treasure's ta'en
        By witchin' skill;
An' dautet twal-pint Hawkie's gane,
        As yell's the bill.

Thence mystic knots mak' great abuse,
On young guidman, fond, keen, an' crouse;
When the best wark-lume i' the house,
        By cantrip wit
Is instant made no worth a louse,
        Just at the bit.

When thowes dissolve the snawy hoord,
An' float the jinglin' icy boord,
Then water kelpies haunt the foor'd
        By your direction,
An' 'nighted travellers are allur'd
        To their destruction.

And aft your moss-traversing spunkies
Decoy the wight that late an' drunk is:
The bleezin', curst, mischievous monkeys
        Delude his eyes,
Till in some rainy slough he sunk is,
        Ne'er more to rise.

Here is the Scottish Devil *par excellence*, the product of popular superstition blended with Calvinist theology.

There is here also the idea which became central to 'Tam o'Shanter' that lone individuals travelling late and having probably drunk far too much are obvious victims for Kelpies and Spunkies. Also in the context of Burns's humour there is a clear indication that it is almost a prerequisite that a late traveller should be drunk in order to be able to see the demons and sprites and that the destruction which befalls them is more than likely due to their inebriation, but the attack by supernatural beings offers a half-way reasonable excuse for what happened should they survive. Burns describes Tam as a consistently heavy drinker especially so on market days: 'That frae November till October, ae market-day thou was nae sober.'

In his poem 'Halloween', Burns produced a compilation of Scottish Lowland folklore with extensive notes by the poet himself. 'Halloween' was composed in 1785.

> Upon that night when faeries light
> On Cassilis Downans dance,
> Or owre the lays, in splendid blaze'
> On sprightly coursers prance;
> Or for Colean the rout is ta'en,
> Beneath the moon's pale beams;
> There up the cove to stray and rove,
> Amang the rocks and streams
>      To sport that night.

Thus goes the first verse of 'Halloween' about which Burns himself wrote in his notes:

Halloween – *is thought to be a night when witches, devils, and other mischief-making beings are all abroad on their baneful midnight errands, particularly those aerial beings, the fairies, are said, on that night, to hold a grand anniversary.*

15

In these notes Burns distances himself somewhat from the superstitions of his countrymen by a process of apparently reporting the thoughts and speech of others with regard to the existence of these 'aerial beings'.

Even the dire superstitions of the past as Burns records their contemporary practice have been watered down to become opportunities for fun and for practising recipes for forecasting fortune usually of a matrimonial nature. No doubt some element of fear and respect for the supernatural still existed and Burns makes great play of this in the behaviour he describes.

For the final great influence on Burns, particularly in the matter of his knowledge of superstition and folklore, we must look to one Betty Davidson who exercised enormous influence in Burns's childhood days. There are many sources of information about this good lady and as in the instances of detail they are sometimes mildly contradictory, I will present most of them here to create a general overview of her influence.

Let us start with the information which resides almost wholly in the realms of legend. When Burns's father was riding for the doctor to assist in Robert's birth, it is related that at the riverside he encountered an old woman, who stopped him and offered her services as midwife. She went back with him to the cottage and stayed some time there, when she was supposed not only to have told the child stories of supernatural beings but also to have prophesied his future–

> The gossip keepit in his loof,
> Quo' she, who lives will see the proof,
> This waly boy will be nae coof;
> I think we'll call him Robin.
>
> He'll use misfortune great an' sma'
> But aye have a heart aboon them a';
> He'll be a credit till us a'
> We'll a' be proud o' Robin.
>
> (from the song 'Rantin', Ravin', Robin')

16

J. Logie Robertson (1904) wrote:

The cottage in which Burns was born stands on the road-side a few yards distant from Alloway Kirk, the central scene of this inimitable tale of drink and diablerie. Now a roofless ruin, the Kirk was, even in Burns's childhood, hoary with age and supernatural associations. 'Many witch stories have I heard,' wrote Burns to Grose the antiquary, 'relating to Alloway Kirk'. These he doubtless 'owed' – it was his own word – to the old woman who resided in the family, remarkable for her ignorance, credulity, and superstition. She had ... 'The largest collection in the country of tales and songs concerning devils, ghosts, faeries, brownies, witches, warlocks, spunkies, kelpies, elf candles, dead lights, wraiths, apparitions, cantrips and other trumpery. These cultivated the latent seeds of poetry, but had so strong an effect upon my imagination that to this hour, in my nocturnal rambles, I sometimes keep a sharp look out in suspicious places.'

> ... while glow'ring round and wi' prudent cares
> Lest bogles catch [me] unawares.

Robertson took this extract from a letter Burns wrote to Dr Moore on the second day of August 1787.

Most of the supernatural beings in Burns's list are well-known but others may not be so familiar. Katharine Briggs (1976) in her book *A Dictionary of Fairies* offered the following definitions of some of the more unfamiliar of these beings.

Brownies (broonies). In the lowlands of Scotland –

They are generally described as small men, about three feet in height, very raggedly dressed in brown clothes, with brown faces and shaggy heads, who come out at night and do the work that has been left undone by servants. They make themselves responsible for the farm or house where they live, reap, mow, thresh, herd sheep, prevent hens from laying away, run errands and give good counsel at need. In return they have the right to a bowl of cream or best milk and to a specially good bannock or cake. They are very easy to offend when they become the mischievous BOGGART. They are afraid of Christian symbols.

Spunkies –

In the lowlands this is the name given to Will o' the Wisp – sometimes believed to be the soul of an unchristened child – usually appears as a fiery devil, who leads people off the road to drown them.

Kelpies – Scottish water horses which haunt rivers –

They can assume human form, that of a rough, shaggy man leaping up behind a solitary rider crushing him almost to death – howls and wails before storms – more usually shaped as a young horse which allowed travellers on to his back then rushing to a deep pool, struck the water with his tail thunderously and disappeared in a flash of light – sometimes believed to tear people to pieces and eat them – when held by a human bridle they could be subdued.

Cantrips – a charm, a spell, an inexplicable trick
Bogles – evil goblins

Robertson believed that it was at Mount Oliphant that Betty Davidson exhibited most of her influence on the young Robert Burns.

It was at Mount Oliphant, too, that the door of the supernatural world opened to the imaginative mind of young Burns. An old relative, Betty Davidson, domiciled in the family, before they left Alloway, had a store of ghostly and ghastly stories, which was exhaust-less, though continually drawn upon. Her disclosure of the apocrypha of the invisible world around him made such a powerful impression on the mind of Robert as to give him, despite the efforts of a singularly robust reason, a permanent belief in its reality, and in its realism as portrayed by old Betty. She, doubtless, was the granny in the Address to the De'il, who was so fearfully intimate with the haunts and habits of the Evil One. And to her certainly we owe the diablerie of Tam o'Shanter.

However Robert Burns in his letter to Dr Moore seems to infer that Betty Davidson was around long before this.
J. Logie Robertson again –

In his autobiographical letter to Dr Moore, Burns writes – 'in my infant days and boyish days I owed much to an old woman who resided in the family, remarkable for her ignorance, credulity and superstition. She had, I suppose, the largest collection in the country of tales and songs concerning devils, ghosts, fairies, witches, kelpies, spunkies, wraiths, apparitions, cantraips ... This cultivated the latent seeds of poetry, which had so strong an effect on my imagination that to this hour, in my nocturnal rambles, I sometimes keep a sharp look out in suspicious places; and though nobody can be more sceptical than I am in such matters, yet it often takes an effort of philosophy to shake off these idle terrors.

That reference to this old woman Betty Davidson and her influence on Burns himself may with some certainty be found in the poem 'Address to the Devil', published in 1784 as suggested by Robertson is to be found in verses 5–6 which go as follows:

> I've heard my rev'rend grannie say
> In lanely glens ye like to stray,
> Or, where auld ruined castles grey
> Nod to the moon,

19

Ye fright the nightly wand'rer's way
            Wi' eldritch croon.

When twilight did my grannie summon
To say her prayers, douce honest woman!
Aft yont the dyke she's heard you bummin
            Wi' eerie drone'
Or, rustlin' through the boor trees, comin'
            Wi' heavy groan.

Gilbert, Robert's brother, wrote of this poem that the curious idea of such an address was suggested to his brother by running over in his mind the many ludicrous accounts and representations we have from various quarters of this august personage. No doubt one of these 'various quarters' and one well placed to influence Burns's thinking on the matter was Betty Davidson herself.

Betty Davidson was actually a cousin of Agnes Burns (*née* Brown), Robert's mother and 'was often the guest of the Burns family for months at a time.' She was a widow, dependent on her son, whose wife treated her very unkindly. Good William Burness consequently had her to stay with them very frequently. Burns says that she had a large collection of tales, songs, and traditions, with which she used to frighten his childish mind; while she was, unconsciously, cultivating his imagination.

When Robert was seven years old his father left Alloway and took the small upland farm of Mount Oliphant and this may have been the end of Betty Davidson's close contact with the growing boy. But without doubt she was one of the main sources of Burns's easy and fluent use of the superstitions and folklore of the supernatural beings which appear in 'Tam o'Shanter' and other poems.

## Robert Burns 1784/6

In February of 1784 Robert Burns's father, a man of some 62 years, died of consumption. The brothers, Robert and Gilbert, decided that they were now free to move from the farm at Lochlie. So having settled all outstanding debts they moved to the tenancy of a farm at Mossgiel about two miles away using what money they were left with as the rent. The village of Mossgiel was also something less than a mile from the market town of Mauchline, which would soon play quite an important part in Robert Burns's life.

The farm that the brothers leased actually belonged to the Earl of Loudon, but was sub-let to Gavin Hamilton who sub-let again to the Burns family. Hamilton was also to become important in the poet's life and not just as his landlord, he eventually became one of Burns's closest friends. Indeed somewhat later Burns used the power of his poetry to decry his friend's treatment by the Kirk Session, as noted earlier.

The farm was roughly 120 acres in extent and the annual rent amounted to £90. The Burns family moved into occupancy on Whit Sunday in 1784.

Robert Burns's sojourn at the farm lasted just two years for several reasons. He started out, as he himself says, 'with full resolution', he read books on farming, tried hard to work out a good routine for running the farm and attended local markets to discuss with, and if possible learn from, the wisdom and practice of the locally established farmers. But, as Gilbert in his notes has recorded, the farm at Mossgiel or Mossgaville '... lies very high and mostly on a cold wet

bottom.' It was not good farming land especially for those without a good deal of experience. It soon became apparent that this lack of experience and practical knowledge in working a farm under these conditions, was to prove disastrous. Robert bought seed stocks of poor quality, the weather was poor and the result was that in their first year half their crops failed.

However, one of the effects of this agricultural incompetence and mischance was that Burns became once more absorbed in his poetry. This must have been some consolation, for he could feel that however poorly he performed as a farmer, he was a gifted poet and becoming a master of his craft.

One of his poems which became public was a splendid defence in verse of his landlord Gavin Hamilton, who was being 'prosecuted' by the Kirk Session for neglect of the Sabbath. The apparent hypocrisy and pettiness of 'Daddy' Auld's action made Burns very angry and this intense feeling flowed over into his next poem 'The Holy Tulzie' or 'The Twa Herds'. The object of his satire and scorn in this case was a quarrel between two reverend Calvinist ministers and resulted in his producing a poem which has been called by Burns himself a 'burlesque lamentation on a quarrel'. These early satires were circulated in manuscript form in the locality and became widely appreciated by certain sections of the community especially those who were part of the growing numbers opposed to the Kirk's dogmatic puritanical assertiveness.

Burns now began to find that his standing in the local community was becoming much more founded upon his growing reputation as a maker of verses than as a farmer. This fact prompted him to continue his onslaught on the hypocrisy, as he saw it, of the local clergy and the extreme orthodoxy of some church members. At this time Burns also became absorbed in the works of his poetic predecessors, for example the Scottish poets Ramsey and Ferguson.

About this time Burns began his love affair with Jean Armour, whose father was a master mason in the town of Mauchline. This affair progressed to the point where in March of 1786, Jean was discovered to be pregnant. When this information was told to her father it is recorded that he fainted. Gilbert informs us that it was intended at this stage that the couple should go through a form of private marriage ceremony after which Robert would leave Jean in the care of her family while he went to Jamaica to work as a bookkeeper on a plantation. It was planned that in this work he would earn enough money to set up his wife and family in a home of their own. Had this actually happened and the poet been away from his native land for a longish period perhaps of several years, it is interesting to speculate on what might have become a vastly different lifestyle and also on what effect this might have had on his poetic inspiration and output.

However, it did not happen!

The lovers had reckoned without Mr Armour! According to Lindsay, James Armour, 'seems to have been a rather dour, churchy kind of man.' He was a member of the Auld Licht section of the church, the more seriously puritanical wing much influenced by Calvinist morality. He was profoundly distressed by his daughter's condition which offended his Calvinist morality but he was also deeply angry at the thought that the man responsible was a penniless poet and incompetent farmer. He was able to obtain hold of the written marriage consent form the two had prepared, usually referred to as 'The unlucky paper' which had been witnessed by a James Smith, and tore Burns's name from the bottom in the belief that by so doing he had succeeded in rendering the contract null and void. There has always been some debate as to whether he was justified in law in believing this to be true. But whether it was or not what really mattered was that Burns believed that Mr Armour's action had essentially destroyed his contract with Jean and indeed had forbidden any further contact with her.

Jean gave birth to twins on 3rd September 1786.

Burns has recorded his sense of desolation at this apparent enforced rejection, but it did not stop his becoming romantically involved with one Mary Campbell who later became the central figure in the poet's most passionate love poem,

'Highland Mary'. Mary Campbell, at the time of her involvement with Burns was in domestic service in the house of Gavin Hamilton though she hailed originally from the Highlands. Burns appears to have met her first in the Spring of 1786; they parted in mid May pledging undying loyalty and fidelity to each other and clearly intending to marry. Sadly they never met again. Mary died in October of that year having contracted a fever in the process of nursing her brother or, as some believe, from the effects of a premature childbirth. She was buried at Greenoch.

The events and people, the passions, sorrows, disappointments and successes of the years 1784/6 seem to have had a stimulating effect on Burns the poet. He produced a great outpouring of work. In 1785 alone among other pieces he produced 'The Jolly Beggars', often regarded as his best work and in competition with 'Tam o'Shanter' for that honour. He also wrote 'Halloween', 'To a Mouse', 'The Cotter's Saturday Night', 'The Addres to the De'il', 'Scotch Drink', and 'Death and Dr Hornbook' all of which appeared in the Kilmarnock edition of his poems with the sole exception of 'Dr Hornbook'.

In 1786 Burns withdrew from the lease of the farm at Mossgiel leaving it entirely to Gilbert and set about preparing a volume of poetry for publication. This appeared in July in Kilmarnock and was entitled, *Poems Chiefly in the Scottish Dialect*. It was printed by J. Wilson. Also at this time Burns was seeking for a job which could be relied upon to provide a better income and more security than he had discovered he could obtain from farming. This is where the idea of Jamaica re-emerged. Through an intermediary he arranged with a Dr Patrick Douglas to take the post of bookkeeper on the doctor's plantation in Port Antonio which was managed by the doctor's brother Charles, for a salary of £30 p.a. He was due to sail from the Clyde in October having booked a passage on *The Nancy*, a brigantine sailing with cargo and passengers to Jamaica, Master Captain Andrew Smith. The price of the ticket for this journey was paid from money he had received from the publication of his book of poems in

24

July. Burns's eagerness to leave Scotland for a job which he may well have found distasteful in its circumstances given his libertarian principles, was probably fuelled by his belief that he was being threatened by legal process initiated by the Armour family over his involvement with their daughter Jean. However, with great benefit to all and to posterity in terms of the work he was able to do later, he did not go. He was advised that before he attempted to earn his living abroad he should take himself and his poetry to Edinburgh. Various influential friends supplied him with letters of introduction. This advice and help which he fortunately took, ultimately led to the poet's wide acceptance by the literati of that city and to the further publication of his poems and to his widespread lionisation.

What charmed his compatriots most in the Kilmarnock edition, there is no question, was his outspokenness, which spared no social sham, no political injustice, derided the pompous 'elected person', proclaimed the dignity of the humblest kind of labour, shot thunderbolts of sly invective and idealism across a landscape sombre with superstitions, social and ecclesiastical.

John Drinkwater

# 2

## DEATH AND DOCTOR
## HORNBOOK

**The Origins of the Poem and its Imagery**

It is often claimed that 'Tam o'Shanter' is the only narrative poem that Burns wrote and indeed that is true. But this poem is sub-titled in some editions of Burns's work, 'A True Story', and though it requires somewhat extensive notes to establish the main background and the essential characters and is thus not a complete, self-contained story like Tam, it is nevertheless, a story in its own right of the imagined meeting of the poet with the apparition of Death, the latter bemoaning the competitive activities of Dr Hornbook.

The implication of truth lies in the fact that Dr Hornbook was the name given by Burns to the local schoolmaster at Tarbolton and the activities of this dominie in purveying quack remedies and medicines, with advice, form the substance of what Death complains of. The pseudo-medical practices were in fact quite real and Burns's poem was believed to have had a devastating effect upon both them and the schoolmaster's classes.

The poem was composed in 1785 at Mossgiel as Burns says 'at seedtime'. As previously noted this work was not included in the Kilmarnock edition of the poems published in July of the following year, but it was printed in the Edinburgh edition of April 1787.

The schoolmaster in question was one John Wilson of Tarbolton the next village to Mauchline. In order to procure additional income to add to his meagre wages as a schoolmaster, Wilson had set up a small shop in the village where he sold groceries. He was a man fascinated by all things medical and had read many of the texts on household medicine and medical practice then available. He then proceeded to add to his sales of goods various drugs and medicaments. He had handbills printed on which, despite his obvious lack of professional training, he advertised that medical advice would be given free in the shop on all common ailments of the village.

In his notes for this poem Burns wrote:

*This gentleman Doctor Hornbook is, professionally, a*

*brother of the Sovreign Order of the Ferula; but, by intui-*
*tion and inspiration, is at once apothecary, surgeon, and*
*physician.*

The reference to the ferula is to the rod with which the
schoolmaster punished unruly or backward pupils. The infer-
ence of quackery is implicit in the title of doctor. The word
'hornbook' is a direct reference in that such was the name
given to a pupil's first school book. It usually consisted of a
page of reading material covered by a layer of translucent
horn which was there to protect the reading page from
becoming soiled or otherwise damaged by the constant
handling of the pupils.

Freemasonry was at the height of its popularity in the last
quarter of the eighteenth century and Burns was a Mason and
had been since 1781 and so was John Wilson. Indeed Wilson
was the secretary of the Tarbolton Masonic Lodge. They met
one evening when they both attended a lodge meeting and the
poet was inadvertently compelled to listen more than a little
impatiently, and certainly not without comment, to the 'baud
apothecary' as he showed off his knowledge and boasted of
his treatment of the village folk and others. Burns realised
that most of Wilson's apparent knowledge was derived from
texts like Buchan's *Domestic Medicine* which had been
published in 1769 and run through many editions, and that
probably not even this was properly understood.

The pair of them left the masonic meeting at the same time
and walked part of the way home together.

Dr John Moore is an important source of information
about Burns. He first became interested in the poet when Mrs
Dunlop sent him a copy of the Kilmarnock edition. On 2nd
August 1787, when ill, Burns wrote what was to come to be
known as 'The Autobiographical Letter' to Dr Moore and the
material it contained has formed the basis of all later accounts
of Burns's life. The poet wrote again to Dr Moore from Ellisland in January 1789 bringing his life story up to date. In the
first letter Burns described how, when he parted from Wilson,
he became aware that his mind was taken up with one of

those 'floating ideas' which set him working all the rest of the way home. The place where he meets Death in the poem, just above 'Willie's mill', was actually the Tarbolton mill run at that time by Willie Muir, was also the place where he actually parted from Wilson on the evening's walk home to Mossgiel. The next afternoon the poem was complete and recited to Gilbert as they worked in their fields. As we have already noted the effect of this poem when published abroad appeared to be quite dramatic. The school run by Wilson lost most of its pupils and customers boycotted his shop. Eventually he was to move to Glasgow where he continued teaching until some time in 1807. He was then appointed a sessions clerk to the Gorbals. In a sense this was fortunate for Wilson because this post was a secure one and indeed proved to be lucrative as well. Lockhart commented that in his later days Wilson used to bless the time when he provoked the wrath of the poet. But it is also recorded that Wilson himself had said, 'I have often wondered what set Robert Burns upon me, for we were aye on the best of terms.' It had apparently not really occurred to him that Burns's attack was motivated by his perception of the damage he was doing with his nostrums and advice to the residents of Tarbolton.

Burns' portrayal of Death in the poem is an interesting combination of the traditional in the use of the skeletal form and original in the fact that the bones are described as being covered with skin from which sprout tufts of hair. Death is also given a beard which is an unaccustomed adornment. From being a terrifying figure as are the leering, contemptuous skeletons of the Dance of Death depictions, Burns has made Death become an object of mockery and derision, particularly by the children. Nevertheless Death's traditional tools, the scythe and the dart are very much in evidence. Death's case against Wilson, in the guise given him by the poet of Dr Hornbook, is quite succinctly put as Robertson in his notes to the poem writes:

... is that the latter cures where the former by long use and wont is entitled to kill, and that he kills where he is not wanted – that is, where the patient would naturally recover if Hornbook did not interfere.

Of the two charges there is no doubt that Burns was much more sympathetic to the second. The description of how the idea floated into his mind is only one of several indications of how Burns conceived some of his poetical works and such descriptions are partly responsible for the assumption often made which gained considerable currency, that his work was instantaneous and complete with little or no need of revision. Indeed this idea was often applied to his creation of 'Tam o'Shanter' despite the evidence that the finished and published work was one of at least three draft ideas. However the Death of his poem was conceived in just such a way and its topicality made an instant impact with the people of Tarbolton so however he came by it the poem was a very successful piece both of imagery and of propaganda.

But it has to be admitted that the belief that Burns's poem forced Wilson to close his shop and flee to Glasgow is almost wholly attributable to Lockhart's account of the matter and there is scant evidence that this is anything other than a gross distortion of the actual facts. Indeed, well after the poem was broadcast there is a record of Wilson asking Burns for advice about applying for a job as a clerk with the Excise.

## Death and Dr Hornbook

(A True Story)

Some books are lies frae end to end,
And some great lies were never penned,
Ev'n ministers, they hae been kenned'
   In holy rapture,
A rousing whid at times to vend'
   And nail't wi' scripture.

But this that I an gaun to tell,
Which lately on a night befell,
Is just as true's the De'il's in hell
   Or Dublin city:
That e'er he nearer comes oursel'
   'S muckle pity.

The clachan yill had made me canty,
I was na fou, but just had planty;
I stachered whyles, but yet took tent aye
   To free the ditches;
An' hillocks, stanes, and bushes, kenned aye
   Frae ghaists an witches.

The rising moon began to glower
Ye distant Cumnockhills out-owre;
To count her horns, wi' a' my power,
   I set mysel',
But whether she had three or four,
   I could na tell.

I was come round about the hill,
And toddlin' down on Willie's mill,
Setting my staff wi' a' my skill,
   To keep me sicker;
Though leeward whyles, against my will,
   I took a bicker.

I there with something did foregather,
That put me in an eerie swither;
An awfu' scythe, out-owre ae shouther,
   Clear danglin', hang;
A three-toed leister on the ither
   Lay, large an' lang.

Its stature seemed lang Scotch ells twa,
The queerest shape that e'er I saw,
For fient a wame it had ava,
   And then its shanks,
They were as thin, as sharp an sma'
   As cheeks o' branks.

'Guid e'en' quo' I; 'Friend ha'e ye been mawin'
When ither folk are busy sowin'?
It seemed to mak' a kind of stan',
   But naething spak',
At length says I, 'Friend, whar ye gaun',
   Will ye go back?'

It spak' right howe – 'My name is Death,
But be na flayed.' Quoth I, 'Guid faith,
Ye're maybe come to stap my breath;
   But tent me billie;
I red ye weel, tak' care o' skaith,
   See, there's a gully!'

'We'll ease our shanks and tak' a seat.'

'Guidman,' quo' he, 'put up your whittle,
I'm no designed to try its mettle;
But if I did, I wad be kittle,
　　　　To be misleard;
I wad na mind it, no, that spittle
　　　　Out-owre my beard.'

'Weel, weel!' says I, 'a bargain be't;
Come gi'es your hand, an' say we're gree't;
We'll ease our shanks an tak' a seat,
　　　　Come gi'es your news;
This while ye ha'e been mony a gate,
　　　　At mony a house.

'Ay, ay!' quo' he an' shook his head,
'It's e'en a lang, lang time indeed
Sin I began to nick the thread,
　　　　An' choke the breath;
Folk maun do something for their bread,
　　　　An' sae maun Death.

'Sax thousand years are near hand fled
Sin' I was to the butching bred,
An' mony a scheme in vain's been laid,
　　　　To stop or scaur' me:
Till ane Hornbook's ta'en up the trade,
　　　　An faith, he'll waur me.

'Ye ken Jock Hornbook i' the clachan,
De'il mak' his kings-hood in a spleuchan!
He's grown sae weel acquaint wi' Buchan
　　　　An' ither chaps.
The weans haid out their fingers laughin'
　　　　An pouk my hips.

'See, here's a scythe, and there's a dart,
That ha'e pierced mony a gallant heart;
But Dr Hornbook, wi' his art
            And cursed skill,
Has made them baith no worth a fart
            Damn'd haet they'll kill.

' 'Twas but yestreen, nae farther gaen,
I threw a noble throw at ane;
Wi' less, I'm sure, I've hundreds slain;
            But de'il-ma-care,
It just played dirl on the bane,
            But did nae mair.

'Hornbook was by, wi' ready art,
And had sae fortified the part,
That when I looked to my dart,
            It was sae blunt,
Fient haet o't wad ha'e pierced the heart
            O' a kail-runt.

'I drew my scythe in sic a fury,
I nearhand cowpit wi' my hurry,
But yet the bauld apothecary
            Withstood the shock;
I might as well ha'e tried a quarry
            O' hard whin rock.

'Even them he canna get attended.
Although their face he ne'er had kenned it,
Just shit in a kail-blade and send it,
            As soon he smells 't,
Baith their disease, and what will mend it,
            At once he yells't.

'And then a' doctors' saws and whittles,
Of a' dimensions, shapes and mettles,
A' kinds o'boxes, mugs an' bottles,
        He's sure to ha'e;
Their Latin names as fast he rattles
        As A, B, C.

'Calces o' fossils, earth, and trees;
True sal-marinum o' the seas;
The farina o' beans and pease,
        He has't in plenty;
Aqua-fortes, what you please,
        He can content ye.

'Dr Hornbook.'
John Wilson drawn from a
silhouette by an unknown artist.

'Forbye some new, uncommon weapons,
Urinus spiritus of capons;
Or mite-horn shavings, filings, scrapings;
            Distilled per se;
Sal-alkali o'midge-tail clippings.
            And mony mae.'


'Wae's me for Johnnie Ged's hole now.'
Quo' I, 'If that news be true!
His braw calf-ward whare gowans grew,
            Sae white and bonnie.
Nae doubt they'll rive it wi' the plew;
            They'll ruin Johnnie!'


The creature grained an eldritch laugh,
And says, 'Ye need na yoke the pleugh,
Kirk-yards will soon be tilled enough,
            Tak ye nae fear;
They'll a' be trenched wi' mony a sleugh
            In twa-three year.


'Whare I killed ane a fair strae-death,
By loss o' blood or want o' breath,
This night I'm free to tak' my aith
            That Hornbook's skill
Has clad a score I' their last claith
            By drap and pill.


'An honest wabster to his trade,
Whase wife's twa nieves were scarce weel-bred,
Gat tippence-worth to mend her head,
            When it was sair;
The wife slade cannie to her bed,
            But ne'er spake mair.

'A countra laird had ta'en the batts,'

'A countra laird had ta'en the batts,
Of some curmurring in his guts
His only son for Hornbook sets,
          An' pays him well.
The lad, for twa guid gimmer pets,
          Was laird himsel.

'A bonnie lass, ye kenned her name,
Some il-brewed drink had hored her wame;
She trusts hersel, to hide the shame,
          In Hornbook's care;
Horn sent her off to her lang hame
          To hide it there.

'That's just a swatch o' Hornbook's way;
Thus goes he on from day to day,
Thus does he poison, kill, and slay,
          An's weel paid for't;
Yet stops me o' my lawfu' prey
          Wi' his damned dirt.

'But, hark! I'll tell you of a plot,
Though dinna ye be speaking o't;
I'll nail the self-conceited sot,
          As dead's a herrin',
Neist time we meet, I'll wad a groat,
          He's get his fairin'!'

But just as he began to tell,
The auld kirk-hammer strak the bell
Some wee short hour ayont the twal,
          Which raised us baith;
I took the way that pleased mysel,
          And sae did Death.

# 3

# THE ADDRESS
# TO THE DE'IL

## The Origins of the Poem and its Imagery

In this particular poem Burns's debt to Betty Davidson and her folk tales, to superstition and images of the supernatural with which she filled him in childhood becomes very obvious.

Robert Inglish wrote, 'Burns had besides another teacher who busily prepared him for his future greatness – an old woman of the neighbourhood, who was a complete storehouse of old ballads and legendary tales, and who so filled the young mind of the poet with stories of witches, and ghosts, and fairies, that even in after life he could scarcely be out alone after nightfall without uneasiness.'

The origins of the Address to the Devil are perhaps to be found in a letter written by Gilbert, Robert's brother, who, living and working the same farm together would have been especially privy to his brother's doings. He wrote, 'It was, I think, in the winter of 1784, as we were going with carts for coals for the family fire (and I could yet point out the particular spot), that Robert just repeated to me the "Address to the De'il". The curious idea of such an address was suggested to him by turning over in his mind the many ludicrous accounts and representations we have had from various quarters of this august personage.'

Robertson wrote:

It embodies the ordinary Scottish peasant conception of the appearance, habits, history and character of the devil. The poem is more or less humorous throughout, but the humour is here dashed with awe, there with imagination; while a sudden infusion of pity and even tenderness flowing unexpectedly and yet naturally from the last stanza, brings the address to a most effective close. I don't think Burns believed in a personal devil – the humorous satire is at the expense of popular Calvinism. The tenderness for an imaginary being, supposed for the moment to be real, who is suffering the pains of eternal misery.

Lindsay wrote:

Scottish poets from Dunbar onwards have adopted a tone of bantering familiarity with the Devil.

Burns was no exception, but as Lindsay goes on to say:

Burns used him (The Devil) to poke fun not only at Scots superstition, but also at the credulity implied by Auld Licht's notions on predestination.

The poem is full of references to Burns's wide reading in the Bible, in Milton and other poets. But it must not be forgotten that Burns held most of the beliefs of his generation, for instance that the world had been created in the year 4004 BC, as witness his use of 6,000 years as the period Death had been dealing with human beings in the thirteenth verse of 'Dr Hornbook'. Such a belief was entirely consonant with the Bible stories of the fall from grace of Satan and for a strong belief in the actual existence of the Devil. Indeed, some in the church held quite strongly that a belief in God was incompatible with disbelief in the existence of the Devil.

In verse four Burns borrows the biblical description of the Devil as, 'going about like a roaring lion seeking whom he may devour'. He also draws on the traditionally accepted role of the Devil as the Prince of the Power of the Air and has him flying with his ghoulish attendants, stripping the roofs of churches, using disinterred bodies in fiendish rituals and for being responsible for most of the apparently inexplicable afflictions and problems which beset mankind.

All the sources available to Burns to add to the list of complaints about the activities of Death are pressed into service. But he also reminds the Devil that he was once beaten in battle by the archangel Michael, a story he drew directly from Milton.

> ... but the sword
> Of Michael from the Armorie of God
> Was giv'n him temperd so, that neither keen

Nor solid might resist that edge: it met
The sword of Satan with steep force to smite
Descending, and in half cut sheere, nor staid,
But with swift wheele reverse, deep ent'ring shor'd
All his right side; then Satan knew pain,
And writh'd him to and fro convolv'd; so sore
The griding sword with discontinuous wound
Pass'd through him, but th'Ethereal substance clos'd
Not long divisible, and from the gash
A stream of Nectarous humor issuing flow'd
Sanguin, such as Celestial spirits may bleed,
And all his Armour stain'd ere while so bright.

Milton *Paradise Lost* Bk VI lines 320/380

**Address to the Devil**

O Prince! O Chief of many throned Powers,
That led th'embattled Seraphim to war.

Milton

O Thou! Whatever title suit thee,
Auld Hornie, Satan, Nick or Clootie,
Wha in your cavern grim and sootie,
          Closed under hatches,
Spaigles about the brunstane cootie,
          To scaud poor wretches.

Hear me, auld Hangie, for a wee,
An' let poor damned bodies be;
I'm sure sma' pleasure it can gie,
          E'en to a de'il,
To skelp an' scaud poor dogs like me,
          An' hear us squeel!

Great is thy power, an' great thy fame;
Far ken'd and noted is thy name;
An though yon lowin heugh's thy hame,
          Thou travels far;
An' faith! Thou's neither lag nor lame,
          Nor blate nor scaur.

'To skelp and scaud poor dogs like me,'

Whyles, ranging like a roarin' lion,
For prey a' holes an' corners tryin';
Whiles on the strong-winged tempest flyin',
        Tirlin' the kirks;
Whyles in the human bosom pryin',
        Unseen thou lurks.

I've heard my reverend Graunie say,
In lanely glens ye like to stray;
Or where auld ruined castles, gray,
        Nod to the moon,
Ye fright the nightly wanderer's way,
        Wi' eldritch croon.

When twilight did my Graunie summon,
To say her prayers, douce, honest woman!
Aft yont the dyke she's heard you bummin'
        Wi' eerie drone;
Or rustlin', through the boortries comin',
        Wi' heavy groan.

Ae dreary, windy, winter night,
The stars shot down wi' sklentin' light,
Wi' you, mysel; I gat a fright,
        Ayont the lough!
Ye like a rash-bush stood in sight,
        Wi' waving sugh.

The cudgel in my nieve did shake,
Each bristled hair stood like a stake,
When wi' an' eldritch stour, quaick-quaick-
        Amang the springs
Away ye squattered, like a drake,
        On whistling wings.

Let Warlocks grim, an' withered hags,
Tell how wi' you on ragweed nags,
They skim the muirs, an' dizzy crags,
             Wi' wicked speed;
And in kirkyards renew their leagues
             Owre howkit dead.

Thence countra wives, wi' toil an'pain,
May plunge an' plunge the kirn in vain;
For oh! the yellow treasure's ta'en
             By witching skill;
An' dawtit twal-pint Hawkie's gaen
             As yell's the bill.

Thence mystic knots mak' great abuse,
On young guidman, fond, keen, an' crouse;
When the best wark-lume i' the house,
             By cantrip wit,
Is instant made no worth a louse,
             Just at the bit.

When thowes dissolve the snawy hoord,
An' float the jingling icy-boord,
The water-kelpies haunt the foord,
             By your direction,
An' 'nighted trav'llers are allured
             To their destruction.

An' aft your moss-traversing Spunkies
Decoy the wight that late an' drunk is;
The bleezing, curst mischievous monkeys
             Delude his eyes,
Till in some miry slough he sunk is,
             Ne'er mair to rise.

'And in kirkyards renew their leagues/Owre howkit dead.'

When Masons' mystic word an' grip,
In storms an' tempests raise you up,
Some cock or cat your rage maun stop,
          Or, strange to tell!
The youngest Brother ye wad whip
          Aff straight to hell!

Lang syne, in Eden's bonnie yard,
When youthfu' lovers first were paired,
An' all the soul of love they shared,
          The raptured hour,
Sweet on the fragrant, flowry swaird,
          In shady bower:

Then you, ye auld, snick-drawing dog;
Ye came to Paradise *incog*,
An' played on man a cursed brogue,
          (Black be your fa' !)
An' gied the infant warld a shog,
          'Maist ruined a'.

D'ye mind that day, when in a bizz,
Wi' reekit duds, and reestit gizz,
Ye did present your smoutie phiz
          'Mang better fo'k';
An' sklented on the man of Uz
          Your spitefu' joke?

An' how ye gat him i' your thrall,
An' brak him out o' house and hall,
While scabs an' blotches did him gall,
          Wi' bitter claw,
An' lowsed his ill-tongued, wicked Scawl',
          Was warst ava?

But a' your doings to rehearse,
Your wily snares an' fechtin' fierce,
Sin' that day Michael did you pierce,
        Down to this time,
Wad ding a Lallan tongue, or Erse,
        In prose or rhyme.

An' now, auld Cloots, I ken ye're thinkin',
A certain Bardie's rantin', drinkin';
Some luckless hour will send him linkin'
        To your black pit;
But faith! He'll turn a corner jinkin',
        An' cheat you yet.

But, fare you weel, auld Nickie-ben!
Oh, wad ye tak' a thought an' men'!
Ye aiblin's might – I dinna ken –
        Still hae a stake –
I'm wae to think upo' yon den,
        Ev'n for your sake!

# 4

# TAM O'SHANTER

## Robert Burns – 1786/91

Wherever English is spoken and moreover where those who speak it are of Scottish descent, the narrative poem 'Tam o'Shanter' is known and loved for its depiction of a roistering farmer, much given up to conviviality, and his desperate meeting with the coven of witches on his way home from Ayr market late on a dark and stormy night. Many of these lovers of the story may never have read Robert Burns's poem, though it is short enough, being only 224 lines long. But, nevertheless, they are almost certain to know of Tam as a 'blethering, blustering drunken blellum,' and his adventures; and they know of Cutty Sark, 'as ae winsome wench and walie,' and of her fiendish pursuit and attack on Tam's grey mare Meg.

There are Burns societies in most cities and towns of the English-speaking world and Burns night, 25th January, is celebrated with due ritual, including a recital of some poems from Burns's *oeuvre* of which 'Tam o'Shanter' is often one.

So what is so enduring and endearing not just about Burns's magnificent poems, songs, and epistles, for after all he is Scotland's national poet, but of the actual tale of a drunken farmer who had an encounter with a witches' sabbat and escaped to tell the tale? What is it about this metrical tale which has brought composers to write music on the theme of Tam's adventure? For instance, Sir A. C. MacKenzie with his Scottish Rhapsody No. 3. of 1911; G. W. Chadwick with 'Tam O'Shanter a Symphonic Ballad' in 1911; F. Learmont

Drysdale wrote 'A Concert Overture of Tam' in 1890; William Harvard Glover composed a piece on Tam for Chorus and Orchestra in 1815; Sir Eugene Goosens wrote a 'Tam O'Shanter Scherzo'; Deryck Cooke composed a piece on Tam for tenor, male chorus, piano and orchestra in 1958 and Malcolm Arnold wrote his rumbustious piece the 'Tam O'Shanter Overture' in 1915. Or for citizens of Scottish descent in the City of Barre in Vermont, USA for example to carve and erect a statue in granite of the poet and on the plinth to carve four panels, two of which are scenes from his poems, one illustrating the action of Meg being pursued by the witches and crossing the Brig of Doon to escape with the loss of her tail (figures 1 and 2); why did Cutty Sark become such a favourite name that in the age of the tea clippers one of the most famous of these magnificent sailing ships was named after her as are many public houses?

Sir Walter Scott said of this particular poem:

This is in many ways the strongest and maturest of all his works ... in Tam o'Shanter Burns surpasses himself: no masterpiece of narrative so concise, so virtuous, so telling, is to be found even in Chaucer. Is it not a strange thing that the king of poetic story-tellers told only one story?

Scott was implying that one of the major assets of Burns's story was the breathtaking speed with which the poem is told and the economy of words which could cover a story with action, description and comment so succinctly employed and with such devastating effect. Scott also said on this score, 'no poet, with the exception of Shakespeare, ever possessed the power of exciting the most varied and discordant emotions with such a rapid transition.'

The story of Tam and Cutty Sark is so simple, it is direct and told with such brilliant brevity but above all with wit and humour. It portrays a lovable rogue; an anxious and harassed wife, Kate, whose homilies on her errant husband's behaviour are so beautifully used to illuminate the character of Tam with

The statue of Robert Burns carved in granite in the city of Barre, Vermont USA.

The base of the statue of Robert Burns at Barre in Vermont USA showing Nannie with Meg's tail in her hand.

all its infuriating weaknesses. The poem also deals with the superstitions and folklore of lowland Scotland in the late eighteenth century with a wry, dry humour and a half belief. While it may be assumed that an individual of Burns's high intelligence would not believe in the 'diablerie' about which he wrote so convincingly, he, as a country farmer was surrounded from early childhood by those who did. It is on record that even later in his life, 'he, could scarcely be out alone after nightfall without an uneasiness.' For instance, in his autobiographical letter to Dr Moore, Burns wrote:

> I sometimes keep a sharp look out in suspicious places, and though nobody can be more sceptical than I am in such matters, yet it often takes an effort of philosophy to shake off these terrors.

Besides 'an effort of philosophy' Burns kept these terrors at bay in 'Tam o'Shanter' by the use of a mocking, wry sense of humour.

Burns was noted for his humour and his somewhat mocking attitude towards those who regarded life as being essentially a serious matter. In a letter to James Smith, a merchant of Mauchline and a close friend, Burns revealed his attitudes to the brevity of human existence and the need to spice life with humour thus:

> But why o' Death begin a tale?
> Just now we're living, sound an' hale;
> Then top and maintop crowd the sail;
>          Heave Care o'er the side!
> And large, before Enjoyment's gale,
>          Let's tak' the Tide.

There are many other examples in Burns's work of his way of poking good-natured fun at the behaviour of his fellows, just as much as there is plain serious intent in his exposure of hypocrisy and of powerful human emotions and sincerity in others. One year he made his tax inventory in verse and the poem 'The Twa Herds' or 'The Holy Tulzie' was about a quarrel between two ministers over their parish boundary. It was handed around between neighbours who must have howled with laughter at the stinging sarcasm and wit with which the poem described the circumstances. Holy Willie's Prayer is often regarded as the most terrible satire in the English language probably written by Burns as revenge on the hypocrite William Fisher who had probably rejoiced to see Burns himself on the penitence stool at the Kirk and had been responsible for reporting Gavin Hamilton, Burns's friend, for getting in his potatoes on the Sabbath and other misdemeanours.

Yet when he came to compose 'Tam o'Shanter', his wife Jean records him, as we shall see later, as walking backwards and forwards by the side of the river near their home, swinging his arms, slapping his thighs and bursting with laughter.

Thus both socially and in terms of folklore Tam rings true. But while many know of Tam and of the gist of his adventures there may be not too many who know the circumstances in which the poem came to be written or of the chance encounter which led to the request for its production. This forms a tale in its own right.

This tale of a poem appears to start in 1789 and it is intimately bound up not just with the life of the poet for the three years until the poem itself was published in 1791, but also with the circumstances of his childhood, his family, and his acquaintances. So although the years 1789–91 are the essential years in the poem's creation it is necessary to appreciate the tale fully to go back much further in the poet's life.

When in 1790 Robert Burns wrote 'Tam o'Shanter' he was 31 years old, farming at Ellisland in Dumfries and had recently taken up an appointment as an exciseman. His marriage to Jean Armour had been acknowledged and legalised and she had borne him a son – their third child – as the twins conceived earlier had died when Jean's parents had refused to accept her in their house.

Jean Armour was the daughter of a master mason of Mauchline and her family had all along disapproved of her relationship with Burns and refused to accept the form of marriage into which the couple had entered earlier. However, when Burns was rejected by the Armour family in the spring of 1785, he prepared himself to emigrate to Jamaica to the plantation of a Dr Douglas. He also wrote one of his most heart-breaking poems 'Highland Mary' based on the life and death of Mary Campbell. This was also the year when the first edition of his poems was published in Kilmarnock on 31st July.

On 28th November of that year following advice, Burns went to Edinburgh and his *Poems* were reviewed by Henry Mackenzie in *The Lounger* on the ninth of December.

Burns was a great social success in Edinburgh. He was welcomed into the world of rank and fashion and well-received by the literary establishment. He had an easy social manner and his intelligence and humour became noted. He was in fact 'lionised'.

During 1786, which turned out to be a very productive year despite its emotionally disastrous start, Burns wrote amongst other things, 'The Twa Dogs', 'The Holy Fair' and 'The Brigs of Ayr'. The following year saw the first Edinburgh edition of the *Poems* which was published on 18th April and was later in the year reprinted twice. It was sold by the publisher and bookseller William Creech.

Burns also undertook a tour of the border counties, beginning in May; of the West Highlands beginning at the end of June, and continued his travels with the Great Tour of the Northern Highlands lasting from the 25th August to 16th September. In the autumn he took an excursion to the Ochils.

Believing, as he later wrote to friends, that he was a single man, because the Armours had refused to accept his association with their daughter Jean, Burns began a relationship with a Mrs M'Lehose, Agnes Craig before her marriage, who was separated from her husband, which occasioned a series of some 60 letters and poems 'to Clarinda' from December but which ended abruptly in March the following year 1788.

During 1787 Burns met a Dr Gregory who was instrumental in opening the way for the poet to take up an appointment with the Excise service, of which he eventually took advantage in 1789.

When Burns returned from Edinburgh and his travels to Mauchline he discovered that his fame and success had completely changed the Armours's attitude to him as a son-in-law. While he was somewhat disgusted by this servile response to his achievements he was still extremely pleased that his relationship with Jean could now be formalised. They were married in May and their wedding confirmed in the church at Mauchline in August of 1788.

Burns now took out a lease on a farm at Ellisland on the banks of the Nith on the estate of Dalswinton near Dumfries and started to establish a home for his wife and child. But his choice of farm had been more directed by its delightful situation than its agricultural merit. He leased the farm from Patrick Miller, brother of Lord Justice Clerk, the lease starting in March. Thus began what was perhaps the happiest period of the poet's life. He had good neighbours and his poetic inspiration flourished. Burns had at last come to a settlement of his financial affairs with Creech his publisher who had been responsible for keeping the poet waiting idly in Edinburgh for payment of his dues. Gilbert, Robert's brother, shared in the funds from the profits of the Edinburgh Edition to the amount of £180 – the rest – some £300, Burns used to furnish the house and stock the farm at Ellisland. He took up residence at the farm in December and he now went to collect Jean whom he had left with her mother at Mauchline. Since Jean had become reconciled with her family Burns had been able to leave her there until he had built the homestead to receive her.

In 1789 in order to supplement his meagre income from the farm, Burns took up the offer of a post as an excise man starting as a 'gauger', a probationer. During his three-and-a-half years spent at Ellisland, Burns wrote 'To Mary in Heaven' in 1789 and 'Tam o'Shanter' the following year. For many reasons as noted earlier the farm did not prosper and as his family increased Burns decided that the farm should become a dairy farm which could be managed by Jean leaving him free to take up his commission in the exercise. His commission as an excise man was received in November 1789 and he received an annual salary of £50 with a hint of possible promotion to Supervisor carrying a salary of £200 per annum. The work was tiring involving riding long distances, often 200 miles per week, with the consequence of prolonged absences from the farm. It was largely these absences from home which led Burns into the habits of 'indiscriminate conviviality'.

In 1790 he wrote 'Tam o'Shanter' as we shall see, largely at the request of Captain Francis Grose whom he had met at the house of his friend and neighbour Robert Riddel the previous year. Ernest Rhys (1921) in his comments on 'Tam o'Shanter' in *The Golden Treasury of Longer Poems* writes:

> This poem was first published in 1791 in the book entitled *Antiquities of Scotland* by Francis Grose. In the preface the author said – 'To my ingenious friend Mr Robert Burns, I have been variously obligated, he was not only at the pains of marking out what was worthy of notice in Ayrshire, the county honoured by his birth, but he also wrote expressly for the work, the pretty tale annexed to Alloway Church.' The pretty tale was Tam o'Shanter. The poem was composed one afternoon in October 1790, whilst the poet was walking by the banks of the river Ellisland.

No doubt Rhys was referring to the finished and eventually published form of 'Tam o'Shanter', for it is recorded that three earlier versions existed as we shall see later.

Burns was, at the time of writing Tam, still at the height of his poetic powers, safe with a guaranteed income, happy in his domestic life and this *joie de vivre* flows into every line of the poem.

In 1791 Burns gave up his farm which had proved unrewarding at Martinmas 11th November and devoted himself solely to being an excise man with a salary of £70 a year. He took up residence in Dumfries in the second storey of a house in the Wee Vennell (Bank Street), where he was apparently easily induced to consort with heavy drinkers. But there is no record that he allowed these habits to affect his work. Nor was there any suggestion of domestic unhappiness.

## Captain Francis Grose

'Tam o'Shanter' would never have been written if Burns had not encountered Captain Grose in the house of his friend Robert Riddell. When the poet discovered that Grose was in the process of collecting information on the antiquities of Scotland and that he was a very proficient artist, he suggested that when Grose started work on his collecting in Ayrshire he should include Alloway Kirk, which had been built around 1516 and last used for worship in 1756, and that he should do a drawing of the Kirk. Burns's overt reason for this request was that Alloway Kirk was his father's place of burial and he hoped might be his also. Knowing that Grose was interested in Scottish folklore and particularly in superstitions, Burns used as an extra persuasion the fact that many stories of witches, spirits, goblins etc. were all linked to the old church as Gilbert Burns later related giving the following account of the most popular of the poet's works.

> When my father feued his little property near Alloway Kirk, the wall of the churchyard had gone to ruin and cattle had free liberty of pasture in it. My father and two or three neighbours joined in an application to the town council of Ayr, who were superiors of the adjoining land, for liberty to rebuild it, and raised by subscription a sum for enclosing this ancient cemetery with a wall: hence he came to consider it as his burial place, and we learned that reverence for it people generally have for the burial

place of their ancestors. My brother was living in Ellis-land, when Captain Grose, in his peregrinations through Scotland, stayed some time at Carse House, in the neighbourhood, with Robert Riddell, of Glenriddell, a particular friend of my brother's. The antiquary and the poet were 'unco pack and thick thegither.' Robert (Burns) requested of Captain Grose, when he should come to Ayrshire, that he would make a drawing of Alloway Kirk as it was the burial place of his father, where he himself had a sort of claim to lay down his bones when they should no longer be serviceable to him; and added, by way of an encouragement, that it was the scene of many a good story of witches and apparitions, of which he knew the captain was very fond. The captain agreed to the request, provided the poet would furnish a witch-story, to be presented along with it. Tam o'Shanter was produced on this occasion and was first published in Grose's Antiquities of Scotland. (1791).

Captain Francis Grose had been born the eldest son of a wealthy jeweller originally from Switzerland, who had designed and created George II's crown and who lived at Richmond. Francis had held a commission of Captain in the Surrey militia, being both Paymaster and Adjutant, but, while still a young man he had become extremely interested in antiquarian research. He studied Art and became proficient at drawing and painting. He had once held the post of Richmond Herald in the College of Arms. When he was about 30 years old he decided to devote the rest of his life, which amounted to some 20 years, to his favourite study. He prepared and published in six volumes the *Antiquities of England and Wales* with some 589 views drawn by the author and 140 plans; and some works on military antiquities before he came to Scotland in the summer of 1789 to write up the antiquities of the northern kingdom; he commenced his work in Dumfriesshire. At this time Robert Burns had been settled for just over a year in his farm of Ellisland, a few miles up the river Nith from Dumfries. Robert Riddell Esq. of Friar's

Carse, a gentleman of antiquarian tastes, was his nearest neighbour about a mile higher up the river, he and Burns had been friends since 1788. It was while dining with Robert Riddell that Burns first met Captain Grose.

Writing from Ellisland on 17th July 1789, Burns said about Grose:

As he has made his headquarters with Captain Riddell, my nearest neighbour, for these three months, I am intimately acquainted with him, and I have never seen a man of more original observation, anecdote, and remark.

Burns and Grose became quite good friends and in 1789 the poet produced a poem about his friend's travels throughout Scotland in search of antiquities. The poem has a mocking, though friendly style, and includes a description of Grose the antiquary.

### Captain Grose's Peregrinations through Scotland.

Hear, Land o'Cakes, and Brither Scots,
Frae Maidenkirk to Johnny Groat's,
If there's a hole in a' your coats,
      I rede you tent it;
A chiel's amang you taking notes,
        And, faith, he'll prent it.

If in your bounds you tend to light
Upon a fine, fat, fodgel wight,
O' stature short, but genius bright,
      That's he, mark weel.
And wow! he has an unco slight
      O' cauk and keel.

In later verses Burns describes Grose as a brave soldier who would fight rather than run but who, having quit the army, has become an antiquarian. He writes of a man who enjoys good company and who has a great sense of fun.

Captain Francis Grose. FSA
Drawn from a Painting by
N. Dance, RA

'Peregrinations' was, as Burns wrote in a letter to R. Graham of Fintry on 9th December 1789, 'the production of my leisure thoughts in my Excise rides'. Burns was appointed to an excise division, in the middle of which lay his farm, about the time of his first acquaintance with Grose in the early autumn. The poem 'Peregrinations' was published in the *Kelso Chronicle* on 4th September 1789 under an assumed name and was later republished in the Scot's magazine for November 1791, and in the Edinburgh edition of his poems in 1793.

Burns so amply fulfilled the accepted condition that he should write a poem to accompany the illustration of Alloway Kirk not only by producing the metrical tale of 'Tam

70

o'Shanter' but also by a letter, (first published by Sir Egerton Brydges in *Censura Literaria* some years after Grose's death), in which he sketched three Kirk Alloway legends. It was the second of these which he eventually elaborated into 'Tam o'Shanter'. In 1790 Grose sent Burns 12 copies of the proof sheets of the poem which the poet distributed to his friends including one to Dr Moore who received it in February 1791 and one to the Reverend Archibald Allison later the same month. To the latter Burns wrote that 'Tam o'Shanter' was his first attempt at telling a tale.

Captain Francis Grose died in Dublin in May 1791. Burns wrote an epitaph:

### On Captain Francis Grose.

The Devil got notice that Grose was a'dying,
So, whip! At the summons old Satan came flying;
But when he approached where poor Francis lay moaning,
And saw each bed-post with its burden a-groaning,
Astonished, confounded, cried Satan, 'By God!
I'll want him, 'ere I take such a damnable load!'

Grose would have been about 50 years old at the time of his death and from the implications of Burns's description of him considerably overweight. But without the chance meeting of Burns and Grose it is very debatable if the former would ever have essayed narrative poetry with such brilliant success.

## Early Versions, Composing and Comments

As noted earlier Burns first met Grose in the summer of 1789, and wrote his peregrinations that year about his new friend's travels, and the bargain about providing a witch story for Grose's book may also have been made at that time. 'Tam o'Shanter' was not published until 1791, and there appears to be no agreed date as to when it was composed but October of 1790 is usually accepted (see Grose). In several records, including that of Carlyle, it was said to have been composed all in one day as the poet strode along the banks of the river by his home. In others, notably that of the Burns's letters there is note of the fact that he actually created three separate and different witch tales about Alloway Kirk. The two records are not incompatible. It is quite probable that if no legends about the kirk were already in existence and were found suitable that Burns had several attempts at drafting a story of his own. He most probably had a year or more from the time of the bargain with Grose in 1789 to October 1790.

He was already supplementing his income by working for the excise and had his recently acquired farm at Ellisland to put in order; he was composing other poems and in a word he was fully employed. For the view of the poem being composed all in one day, Lockhart writes of an afternoon in October 1790:

> This poem is said to have been the work of one day, and
> Mrs Burns well remembers the circumstances. He spent

most of the day on his favourite walk by the river, where in the afternoon she joined him with some of her children. He was busily engaged crooning to himself; and Mrs Burns, perceiving that her presence was an interruption, loitered behind with their little ones among the broom. Her attention was presently attracted by the strange and wild gesticulations of the bard, who, now at some distance, was agonised with an ungovernable access of joy. He was reciting very loud, and with the tears rolling down his cheeks, the lines:

'Now Tam! O Tam! had they been queans.

To the last Burns was of the opinion that 'Tam o'Shanter' was the best of his poems. There is little doubt that Burns did compose 'Tam o'Shanter' on that October day in an ecstasy of humour and inspiration. But there is equally little doubt that he had gone through the process of drafting at least two other ideas and indeed written them down or there would have been no source material to be published after Grose's death by Sir Egerton Brydges. This letter, presumably originally addressed to Grose to give him some indication of what the poet had in mind, as noted contained three versions, the second of which was elaborated into 'Tam o'Shanter' and the third had been claimed by some authorities to have inspired Hogg (1770–1835), the Ettrick Shepherd's, metrical story of drink and diablerie *The Witch of Fife*.

The text of the second of the Alloway sketches is as follows:

On a market day in the town of Ayr a farmer from Carrick, and consequently whose way lay by the very gate of Alloway Kirk yard, in order to cross the river Doon at the old bridge, which is about two hundred or three hundred yards further on than the said gate, had been detained by his business, till by the time he reached Alloway it was the wizard hour between night and morning. Though he was terrified with a blaze streaming from the Kirk, yet, as it is a well-known fact that to turn back on these occasions is running up by far the greater risk of mischief, he prudently advanced on his road. When he reached the gate of the kirk-yard he was surprised and entertained, through the ribs and arches of an old Gothic window, which still faces the doorway, to see a dance of witches merrily footing it around their old, sooty, blackguard master, who was keeping them all alive with the power of his bagpipe. The farmer, stopping his horse to observe them a little, could plainly descry the faces of many old women of his acquaintance and neighbourhood. How the Gentleman was dressed tradition does not say – but that the ladies were all in their smocks; and one of them happening unluckily to have a smock which was considerably too short ... our farmer ... burst out with a loud laugh. Weel lumpen, Maggy wi' the short sark! and recollecting himself, instantly spurred his horse to the top of his speed. I need not mention the universally known fact that no diabolical power can pursue you beyond the middle of a running stream. Lucky it was for the poor farmer the river Doon was so near, for, not withstanding the speed of his horse, which was a good one, against he reached the middle of the arch of the bridge, and consequently the middle of the stream, the pursuing vengeful hag was so close at his heels that one of them actually sprang to seize him; but it was too late; nothing was on her side of the stream but the horse's tail, which immediately gave way at her infernal grasp, as if blasted by a stroke of lightning; but the farmer was beyond her reach ... However, the unsightly tailless condition of the vigorous steed was, to the last hour of the noble creature's life, an awful warning to the farmers not to stay too late in Ayr markets.

Not all the elements of the 'Tam o'Shanter' story are present in this sketch. For instance, there is no indication of the farmer's drunken behaviour, nor of his wife's suffering. But above everything else the character of the farmer and of the witch with the short shift are almost entirely missing. It is no wonder that when Burns came to turn this somewhat cold and prosaic tale into the magic of 'Tam o'Shanter' in the marvellously expressive Scots vernacular that he should have demonstrated a great elation as it all pulled together so well.

There have been several attempts over the years to establish a possible role model for Tam – but they are at best extremely speculative. Shanter was a farm in Carrick on the south shore of Ayrshire at the time 'Tam' was written. It was tenanted by one Douglas Graham who may or may not have contributed some characteristics to Robert Burns's Tam. It matters little, for Tam is wholly the creation of a poet with a deep and intelligent understanding of human behaviour especially of those among whom he lived all his life. There has also been speculation that a man called John Davidson had been used by Burns as the prototype of Souter Johnnie. Davidson lived near the farm called 'Shanter' and was indeed a shoemaker. He was also known to be quick-witted and the poet was a frequent visitor to his house.

Another character in 'Tam o'Shanter', Kirkton Jean, is usually identified with Jean Kennedy who, with her sister Anne, was the joint proprietor of a small inn in the kirk town of Kirkoswald. The sisters were respectable people and were known locally as 'The Leddies' and their inn as 'The Leddies' House' rendered by Burns in 'Tam o'Shanter' as 'The Lord's House'.

In a letter dated 11th August 1791 to Mrs Dunlop, Burns wrote: 'I look on Tam o'Shanter to be my standard performance in the poetical line.'

In the estimation of the general public 'Tam o'Shanter' was certainly Burns's best work. This was also the opinion of Sir Walter Scott and of John Gibson Lockhart who published a life of Burns in 1828. Thomas Carlyle and Matthew Arnold were of the opinion that the 'Jolly Beggars' was a better poem. Indeed Carlyle was sufficiently critical of 'Tam' to say, 'It is not so much a poem as a piece of sparkling rhetoric.' He also complained that the poem did not hold together:

The strange chasm which yawns in our incredulous

imaginations between the Ayr public house and the gate of Tophet, is nowhere bridged over, nay the idea of such a bridge is laughed at; and thus the tragedy of the adventure becomes a mere drunken phantomasgoria or many coloured spectrum painted on ale-vapours, and the farce alone has any reality. (Essay on Burns.).

In essence Carlyle's harsh comments on 'Tam o'Shanter' may have as much to do with their author's efforts to counterbalance what he considered to be Sir Walter Scott's too strong and biased praise for the poem. For amongst other claims for the poem, Scott, who had met Burns during his brief period in Edinburgh, had said:

In Tam o'Shanter, Burns surpasses himself: no masterpiece of the narrative is so concise, so various, so telling, is to be found even in Chaucer. Is it not a strange thing that the king of poetic story tellers told only one story?

But Carlyle's comments were by no means all highly critical especially when directed not at any specific work by Burns but at his standing as a poet:

He has found a tone and words for every mood of man's heart

and again:

strictly speaking, perhaps no British man has so deeply affected the thoughts and feelings of so many men, as the solitary and altogether private individual, with means apparently the humblest. (Essay on Burns).

## Tam o'Shanter
A Tale

'Of Brownys and Bogillis full is this buke.'
Gavin Douglas (1474–1522)

When chapman billies leave the street,
And drouthy neibors neibors meet,
As market-days are wearing late,
An' folk begin to tak' the gate;
While we sit bousing at the nappy,
An' getting fou and unco happy,

We think na on the long Scots miles,
The mosses, waters, slaps, and styles,
That lie between us an our hame,
Where sits our sulky, sullen dame,
Gathering her brows like gathering storm,
Nursing her wrath to keep it warm.

'Where sits our sulky, sullen dame'

This truth fand honest Tam o'Shanter,
As he frae Ayr ae night did canter
(Auld Ayr, whom ne'er a town surpasses
For honest men and bonny lasses).

O Tam! hadst thou been sae wise
As ta'en thy ain wife Kate's advice!
She tauld the weel thou was a skellum,
A bletherin', blusterin', drunken blellum,
That, frae November till October,
Ae market-day thou was na sober;
That ilka melder, wi' the miller,
Thou sat as lang as thou had siller;
That every naig was ca'd a shoe on –
The smith and thee gat roaring fou on;
That at the Lord's house, even on Sunday,
Thou drank wi' Kirkton Jean till Monday.
She prophesied that, late or soon,
Thou wad be found deep drown'd in Doon;
Or catch'd wi' warlocks in the mirk,
By Alloway's auld haunted kirk.

'She tauld thee thou was a skellum'

Ah! gentle dames! it gars me greet
To think how mony counsels sweet,
How mony lengthen'd sage advices,
The husband frae the wife despises!

But to our tale. Ae market night
Tam had got planted unco right
Fast by an ingle, bleezing finely,
Wi' reaming swats, that drank divinely;
And at his elbow, Souter Johnnie,
His ancient, trusty, drouthy crony;
Tam lo'ed him like a very brither;
They had been fou for weeks thegither.
The night drave on wi' songs an clatter;
And aye the ale was growing better:
The landlady and Tam grew gracious,
Wi' favours, secret, sweet, and precious:
The souter tauld his queerest stories;
The landlord's laugh was ready chorus:
The storm without might rair and rustle,
Tam did na mind the storm a whistle.

Care, mad to see a man sae happy,
E'en drowned himsel' amang the nappy.
As bees flee hame wi' lades o' treasure,
The minutes wing'd their way wi' pleasure:
Kings may be blest, but Tam was glorious,
O'er a' the ills o' life victorious.

But pleasures are like poppies spread –
You seize the flower, its bloom is shed!
Or like the snow falls in the river –
A moment white – then melts for ever;
Or like the borealis race –
That flit ere you can point their place;
Or like the rainbow's lovely form –
Evanishing amid the storm.

Nae man can tether time or tide;
The hour approaches, Tam maun ride;
That hour, o' night's black arch the keystane,
That dreary hour Tam mounts his beast in;
And sic a night he tak's the road in
As ne'er poor sinner was abroad in.

The wind blew as 'twad blawn its last;
The rattling showers rose on the blast;
The speedy gleams the darkness swallow'd;
Loud, deep, and lang the thunder bellow'd:
That night a child might understand,
The de'il had business on his hand.

Weel mounted on his grey meare, Meg,
A better never lifted leg,
Tam skelpit on thro' dub and mire,
Despising wind and rain and fire –
Whiles holding fast his gude blue bonnet,
Whiles crooning o'er an auld Scots sonnet;
Whiles glow'ring round wi' prudent cares
Lest bogles catch him unawares.
Kirk-Alloway was drawing nigh
Where ghaists and houlets nightly cry.

'Tam skelpit on thro' drub and mire'

By this time he was cross the ford,
Whare in the snaw the chapman smoor'd:
And past the birks and meikle stane,
Whare drunken Charlie brak's neck-bane:
And thro' the whins, and by the cairn,
Where hunters fand the murder'd bairn:
And near the thorn, aboon the well,
Where Mungo's mither hanged hersel'.
Before him the Doon pours all his floods:
The doubling storm roars through the woods;
The lightnings flash from pole to pole:
Near and more near the thunders roll:
When, glimmering thro' the groaning trees
Kirk-Alloway seem'd in a bleeze;
Through ilka bore the beams were glancing;
And loud resounded mirth and dancing.

'Before him the Doon pours all his floods'

Inspiring bold John Barleycorn
What dangers thou canst mak' us scorn!
Wi' tipenny we fear nae evil;
Wi' usquebae we'll face the devil!
The swats sae reamed in Tammie's noddle,
Fair play – he car'd na de'ils a boddle!
But Maggie stood right sair astonished,
Till, by the heel and hand admonished,
She ventur'd forward on the light;
And, Wow! Tam saw an unco sight!

'And, Wow! Tam saw an unco sight!'

Warlocks and witches in a dance:
Nae cotillion, brent new frae France.
But hornpipes, jigs, strathspeys and reels,
Put life and mettle in their heels.
At winnock-bunker in the east,
There sat auld Nick in shape o' beast
A towzie tyke, black, grim and large!
To gi'e then music was his charge:
He screw'd the pipes and gart them skirl
Till roof and rafters a' did dirl!
Coffins stood round, like open presses,
That shaw'd the dead in their last dresses;
And, by some devilish cantrip sleight,
Each in its cauld hand held a light,
By which heroic Tam was able

'There sat auld Nick in shape o' beast'

To note upon the haly table,
A murderer's banes in gibbet airns;
Twa span-lang, wee, unchristen'd bairns;
A thief new-cutted frae a rape –
Wi' his last gasp his gab did gape;
Five tomahawks wi' blude red-rusted;
Five scimitars wi' murder crusted;
A garter which a babe had strangled;
A knife a father's throat had mangled,
Whom his ain son o' life bereft –
The grey hairs yet stack to the heft;
Wi' mair of horrible and awfu',
Which ev'n to name wad be unlawfu'.

'A thief new-cutted frae a rape'

As Tammie glower'd, amaz'd and curious,
The mirth and fun grew fast and furious:
The piper loud and louder blew;
The dancers quick and quicker flew;
They reel'd, they set, they cross'd, they cleekit,
Till ilka carlin swat and reekit,
And cast her duddies on the wark,
And linket at it in her sark.

Now Tam, O Tam! Had they been queans
A' plump and strapping in their teens,
Their sarks, instead o' creeshie flannen,
Been snaw-white seventeen hunder linen;
Thir breeks o' mine, my only pair,
That ance were plush, o' guid blue hair,
I wad hae gi'en then off my hurdies,
For ae blink o' the bonnie burdies.

But wither'd beldams, auld and droll,
Rigwoodie hags wad spean a foal,
Louping an' flinging on a crummock,
I wonder didna turn thy stomach.

'Louping an' flinging on a crummoch'

But Tam kent what was what fu' brawlie:
There was ae winsome wench and waulie,
That night inlisted in the core,
Lang after kenn'd on Carrick shore!
(For mony a beast to dead she shot,
And perish'd mony a bonnie boat,
And shook baith meikle corn and bear,
And held the country-side in fear).
Her cutty-sark, o' Paisley harn,
That while a lassie she had worn,
In longitude tho' sorely scanty,
It was her best, and she was vauntie.
Ah! little kent thy reverend grannie,
That sark she coft for her wee Nannie
Wi' twa pund Scots ('twas a' her riches)
Wad ever grac'd a dance o' witches!

'To sing how Nannie lap an flang,'

But here my muse her wing maun cour;
Sic flights are far beyond her power –
To sing how Nannie lap an flang
(A souple jade she was and strang)
And how Tam stood, like ane bewitch'd,
And thought his very e'en enrich'd!
Even Satan glowr'd, and fidg'd fu' fain,
And hotch'd and blew wi' might and main;
Till first ae caper, syne anither,
Tam tint his reason a' thegither,
And roars out 'Weel done, Cutty Sark!'
And in an instant all was dark;
And scarcely had he Maggie rallied,
When out the hellish legion sallied.

'When out the hellish legion sallied.'

'As bees bizz out wi' angry fyke'

As bees bizz out, wi'angry fyke
When plundering herds assail their byke;
As open pussie's mortal foes
When pop! she starts before their nose;
As eager runs the market-crowd
When, 'catch the thief' resounds aloud;
So Maggie runs, the witches follow,
Wi' mony an eldritch skriech and hollow.

'So Maggie runs, the witches follow'

Ah, Tam! ah, Tam! thou'll get thy fairin'!
In hell they'll roast thee like a herrin'!
In vain thy Kate awaits thy comin' –
Kate soon will be a woefu' woman!
Now do thy speedy utmost, Meg,
And win the keystane o' the brig;
There at them thou thy tail may toss,
A running stream they dare na cross.
But ere the keystane she could make
The fient a tail she had to shake.

For Nannie, far before the rest,
Hard upon noble Maggie prest,
And flew at Tam wi' furious ettle;
But litle wist she Maggie's mettle!
Ae spring brought off her master hale,
But left behind her ain grey tail;
The carlin claught her by the rump,
And left poor Maggie scarce a stump!

'And left poor Maggie scarce a stump!'

Now, wha this tale o' truth shall read,
Each man and mother's son, take heed:
Whene'er to drink you are inclined,
Or cutty sarks rin in your mind,
Think! – ye may buy the joys o'er dear;
Remember Tam o' Shanter's meare.

# EPILOGUE

Virtual reality is a common enough twenty-first century phenomenon. Its main claim to interest lies in the technique of giving apparent reality to things which are in fact of a different order of reality usually by the creation of images electronically which, by paying great attention to the presentation of accurate detail and the illusion of three dimensionality, deceive the perception of an observer or participant into a belief that they are in a particular environmental situation and part of the events taking place there. The process is a rather more thorough and encompassing illusion than had heretofore been possible and may include all the sensory inputs. Burns created a verbal virtual reality for his audiences of beings and their environment which had previously only existed in their imaginations based upon a common and low level communication. He produced from the realms of imagination creatures which, by employing fully his powerful descriptive skills and by using a common language, acquired a new and vivid existence, a virtual reality.

We, who are surrounded and bombarded by created images from television, film, and advertising can only find it very difficult to imagine what the effect Burns's recreation of these images of fear had upon his readers and hearers. Their images had been developed from the words of the preachers they had listened to for whom pictures of hell and damnation were a potent instrument of exacting religious conformity; from the folk tales and traditions which circulated by word of mouth and by common practice, and Burns had now taken these crude images, refined and fixed them much more vividly and clearly than his audiences could ever have achieved for themselves. That he also introduced an element of mockery into the process would have added to the potency of the images and their ready acceptance.

Burns, like Shakespeare, had the gift of an intuitive psychology, what amounts to an understanding of human existence and behaviour at a level that was uncommon at a time when most people implicitly believed that they had conscious control over their behaviour and were in fact responsible for its consequences except in so far as they were influenced by powerful mystical forces over which they had no power of control or to resist but merely to accept and appease. Long before psychologists were aware of how self-identity was established, Burns was commenting in his verse on the need for individuals to see themselves through the eyes of others who were important to them and noting that the general lack of this ability was one of the prime causes of misunderstanding between people and of relational conflict. Indeed, the other aspect which 'Tam o'Shanter' emphasises is the consequence of certain kinds of social behaviour especially in the relationship between husband and wife and what nowadays would be called the 'male bonding' of the convivial male drinking session.

If Burns needed supernatural imagery to help make his point about drunkenness, he did it with a light touch and, as is evident from his later life, was quite capable of ignoring his own message in his own behaviour.

We have to remember that each of the poems under consideration here was written for a specific purpose. 'Halloween', which contains the least supernatural imagery of the four, was written to meet Burns's desire to record the activities of that particular night which were, even at that time, fast becoming rituals almost without meaning; 'Dr Hornbook' was written as a matter of social conscience, an exposure of potentially harmful quackery but probably also as a mild form of revenge for having had to listen to an extended bout of boasting by his fellow mason, Wilson; 'The Address', according to Gilbert Burns, was born from Robert's musings on the wide variety of images and names that was in current use about the Devil and his machinations against humankind. 'Tam' is the only work of the four that was effectively commissioned. It was written, as we have seen, to provide illustration of the legends associated with Alloway old kirk at the request of the antiquarian Francis Grose, to be included in his survey of the antiquities of Scotland.

It is not in the least surprising that 'Tam' became so popular, but because its original purpose was not so well known its popularity as a rollicking good yarn has tended to create a sense among those who know little of Burns's other work, that the poet was overly concerned with ghosties, ghoulies, bogles and witches, when such is far from the case. Indeed Burns's references to the supernatural and of images based upon it are few but none the less remarkable for that.

In three of the four poems in which Burns uses supernatural imagery the language he employs is the common vernacular Scots of the lowlands of his homeland. The reason for this usage is manifestly obvious and is not as some critics have implied that he was unable to write 'good' English, but rather because the message which he intended to convey was addressed principally to people who spoke that vernacular in their everyday lives and indeed thought in it. To be able to reach people in this way it is necessary not only to be able to use a known and familiar set of symbols, but also to have knowledge of the thought processes, prejudices and belief systems of the proposed recipients. Burns was quite able to think in the same way as the people he wanted to address, but he could also by virtue of his intelligence and the avid search for knowledge which had occupied a great deal of his childhood and early manhood, think in an entirely different way – a way which gave him the detachment and the clarity of vision of the outsider watching others while still having the 'gut' feelings of those he addressed. It is very clear that Burns was well aware of his semi-detached observer status and was thus able to quickly note its presence in the behaviour of others. For instance, he described his friend Grose, who came from a background essentially very different from that of the poet, as a child come among the locals and taking notes who would miss nothing. The image of a child as used here is one of innocence – not lack of knowledge or experience – but of the open receptivity of a child's mind as he/she is daily faced with new and different experiences.

In the poem 'Halloween' Burns uses a vocabulary which is almost as old as the decaying traditions he portrays with it. J. Logie Robertson (1904) comments:

It contains a larger proportion of old Scottish words than

any other piece he has composed. Many of these words are now all but obsolete, and some of them even in Burns's day were comparatively rare. But there was merit in using them.

He went on to note that Hamilton of Gilbertfield writing to Allan Ramsay said of his use of the same kind of language

... thy bonnie auld words gar me smile.

Burns was aware, like all effective creative artists, that the choice of the materials of expression was an essential part of the process of conveying his message.

Although Burns in his 'autobiographical letter' to Dr Moore expressed concern about his ability to write in English e.g. '... my scarcity of English denies me the power of doing her justice in that language ...', he was referring in this instance to his verses on Nelly Kirkpatrick, his partner in the hayfield when he was 16; he soon acquired a competent skill in the use of eighteenth-century English which he was to use often when he felt that the subject matter of what he was writing was addressed to those who commonly used this form of speech or when he felt that he needed to demonstrate his rich store of learning. On occasions he had as Robertson writes: '... a weakness in his English composition for a word of "learned length".'

The supernatural element in the poem 'Halloween' is slight when compared to the other three works discussed here. It was apparently written about the time of Halloween in 1785 and comprises a description of various traditional rites which are performed at that time, most of which take the form of invoking the encircling spirits to reveal the future and in particular the matrimonial future. Burns's own introductory note explains:

The following poem will, by many readers, be well enough understood; but for the sake of those who are unacquainted with the manners and the traditions of the country where the scene is cast, notes are added, to give some account of the principal charms and spells of that night, so big with prophecy to the peasantry in the west of Scotland. The passion of prying into futurity makes a striking part of the history of human nature in its rude state, in all ages and nations; and it may be some entertainment to a philosophic mind, if any such should honour the Author with the perusal, to see the remains of it among the more unenlightened in our own.

Whether Burns was aware of it or not, 'Halloween' has performed the role of recording the state to which ancient Celtic ritual had deteriorated by the late eighteenth century and, as some have noted, without it many such customs would have lapsed into obscurity. The last statement of Burns's introductory comment would seem to indicate that not only was he aware that the rites performed by his contemporaries were but a sorry shadow of the original rituals fuelled more by a need to foretell the future with some apprehension that there may be spirits in actual existence than having any understanding of the proceedings as the embers of a religion of natural forces, but also he seems to have believed that they would soon be completely eradicated as rational thought replaced superstition. He was of course right up to a point, but he cannot ever have imagined the half-fearful superstitious spell-making of his contemporaries would be replaced not by rationality but by the semi-commercial enterprise of frightening people into contributing money or gifts to the frighteners or face the possibility of some penalty as in the trivialised process of the modern trick or treat, which is in essence a minor form of extortion masquerading under the guise of fun.

The rational processes which Burns believed would eradicate superstition have not performed as he would have wished – superstition is as rife in our society as it was in his – but it takes some different forms. Indeed had Burns pursued his insights into his own mind where he was aware of the influence that superstition had upon himself and equally aware of how his ability to think rationally and logically co-existed with a half-belief in the supernatural, he would have realised that humans will always have fear of the unknown and more particularly of the unknowable and will tend to transfer the process of coping from other aspects of their lives in order to deal with them in despite of logic.

There are only two distinct references to supernatural beings in the whole poem though the presence of others is inferred throughout. In the first line there is a reference to fairies and in the notes to verse 21 Burns writes:

You go to the barn, and open both doors, taking them off the hinges if possible; for there is a danger that the being about to appear may shut the doors and do you some mischief.

Prying into futurity may have been fun, but part of that fun which Burns realised quite well, was that the participants were not entirely sure whether there was an element of potential danger or not.

O Death! Thou tyrant fell and bloody!
The meikle devil wi' a woodie
Haurl thee hame to his bleak smiddie
        O'er hurtcheon hides,
And like stock-fish come o'er his studdie
        Wi' thy auld sides.

This is the opening stanza of Burns's 'Elegy on Captain Matthew Harrison', and contains another reference to the poet's image of Death and the Devil. The verse expresses the wish that Death should be hauled by a rough rope over the spines of hedgehogs to Hell. By implication, Death, though skeletal, is not just bones but is a shrivelled up figure whose skin, Burns hopes, will still retain sufficient sensitivity to feel the torment of being dragged over the spines of the hedgehogs. Indeed, Burns compares Death's body to that of a dried fish and hopes that when the Devil gets his prey back to Hell he

114

will use the dried up body as a hammer and smash it on the anvil in his forge.

In essence the figure of Death in this elegy is very similar to the physical appearance which the poet gives to Death in the Hornbook tale; but here the dried fish analogy serves to display Burns's erudition. He obviously knew that the word 'skeleton' was derived from the Greek word 'skeletos' and he also knew that it meant 'dried up'. The uses of the image of Death in the Hornbook tale are varied. Burns was making the point that Wilson was a charlatan in the very obvious sense that he had no training in the matter of the administration of medicines. Death, always a fearful prospect for humans, he makes into a figure of fun mocked by the local children. But by doing so he makes the very solid point that if Death, who might have been expected to relish Wilson's activities in practising medicine for the greater number of victims he might have created, was more hurt in his professional pride by the fact of a mere human usurping his role, then Wilson's behaviour had to be very scandalous. In the process Burns succeeded in making death a less terrifying figure, was able to emphasise the enormity of Wilson's exploitation of the gullible and destroyed the schoolmaster's credibility. Apart from this he also demonstrated that the representation of what was a natural expectation of any creature that had life as a skeletal figure wielding a dart and a trident as portrayed by the Calvinist preachers was a myth perpetuated to frighten the credulous. Whether his effort to get the figure of death accepted as an anthropomorphic personification and thus a move towards accepting death as a rational reality may well be dubious. The imagery of fear is very hard to eradicate.

The origins of the use of a skeletal figure to represent Death may, in this country, have first appeared shortly after the christianisation in the seventh and eighth centuries. The earliest representations of Death for common consumption appear to have occurred as part of a pageant organised by the church, in which the participants were dressed as all the ranks in society and each in turn was snatched from the proceedings by another person dressed as the individual's corpse. In a copy of *The Dance of Death* illustrated by Holbein there is written by an unknown hand:

> ... in the dark ages of monkish bigotry and superstition, the deluded people, terrified into a belief that the fear of death was acceptable to the great Author of their existence, had placed one of their principal gratifications in contemplating it amidst ideas the most horrid and disgusting: hence the frequent descriptions of mortality in all its shapes amongst their writers, and the representations of this kind, in their books of religious offices, and the paintings and sculptures of their ecclesiastical buildings.

It would seem that about the middle of the fourteenth century the 'corpse' of the pageant became a skeleton who led all, from the pope to the pauper, away from the land of the living. Langland in his *Visions of Piers Plowman* composed about 1350 wrote:

> Death came dryvinge after, and all to dust pashed,
> Kynges and Kaysers, knightes and popes
> Learned and lewde, he let no man stande
> That he hitte even, he never stode after.

The burgeoning of Death as an image possessing a virtual reality as a skeletal figure occurred during the fifteenth and sixteenth centuries when wall paintings of Death leading off individual figures or a succession of figures in what came to be known as the Dance of Death, sculpture, stained glass windows and, when printing flourished, in books and leaflets as well, proliferated. They were alternatively known as the *Danse Macabre*, a term which is unreliably reported as having derived from a German poet of the early fifteenth century who wrote of Death taking all regardless of rank. But the word '*macabre*' seems much more reliably to have arisen from the medieval miracle plays in which the slaughter of the Maccabees was represented in Old French as '*Danse Macabree*'.

Burns's depiction of Death, while soundly based in ancient tradition, has its own unique touches in that the skeletal structure is covered with a dried and shrivelled skin; the skull has a beard and the skin an eruption of tufts of coarse hair. I can find no origin for these anomalies and can only assume that they were created by Burns himself though in Dürer's woodcut 'Death and the Landsknecht', not only is Death a skeletal figure carrying an hour glass but also sports a head of shaggy hair. Their purpose is not far to seek. While not wanting to waste the symbol of the skeletal figure, Burns did not want his death to be a terrifying image but one that would attract mockery and probably a certain amount of sympathy. If the result was as we are assured that it was, then he succeeded. Burns was an obviously extremely effective contriver of images which he knew how to use to achieve maximum effect on his audiences and readers.

Burns's imagery of the Devil is found in the Address, in 'Tam o'Shanter' and also briefly in the 'Elegy on Captain Matthew Harrison' as just noted. In his introduction to the paperback edition of the *Malleus Maleficarum*, originally written by Kramer and Sprenger somewhere around 1486, Dennis Wheatley writes:

But as time went on, largely owing to the Romantic appeal of the Crusaders, more and more people abandoned their Pagan beliefs, and the church succeeded in transforming the jovial, benign Horned God into Satan. Not in his original form as the beautiful, rebellious archangel 'Lucifer, Son of the Morning' but as a newly created horror with horns, hoofs and a spiked tail, an insatiable lover of licentious women and the inspirer of all evil, whom they named 'The Devil'.

It is that latter image which Burns uses most effectively though, as he demonstrates, he is aware of the other image of Lucifer in his reference to Milton in the Address. In a way that reference does not fit too well with all the other descriptive lines which have the Devil as black, sooty and living in a burning cavern, he is the tormentor of mortals, the destroyer of churches, he pries into human affairs, he flies across the moors with a retinue of witches, he is a despoiler of the graves of the newly dead and the promoter of the hurtful and mischievous activities of others of his legions of creatures. The fire and forge of the Devil's workshop appear in the Harrison elegy and these seem to have derived from the age-long connection that people have always made between the blacksmith and the otherworld and spirits.

The Devil of 'Tam o'Shanter' is a strange confection. It has always been believed by the credulous that it was possible for the devil to appear to mortals in whatever form he chose and a large black dog is not an uncommon manifestation – but one that plays the bagpipes? The whole sordid and horrible seriousness of devil worship is dissolved in this description and the Devil becomes, as Burns intended he should, a figure to be mocked and laughed at. Indeed all the horrors with which Burns strews Tam's journey through the night, are all occasioned by human activity not the Devil's; a suffocation; a broken neck; a murdered child; a hanging. Of course it is possible to argue that these events, though all of human agency, were inspired by the presence of evil. The 'horrible and awfu', on the altar are also symbolic of human violence rather than of devilish activity and yet Burns knows well enough that the horror of their presence in his story will transfer to all the other aspects of it.

The witches in 'Tam o'Shanter' are not strictly speaking supernatural beings at all, indeed as Burns portrays them they are old, ugly recognisable denizens of the area, and deranged worshippers of Auld Clootie. That is with the exception of Nannie who, while being equally misguided as her colleagues, is still young and supple. It is debatable whether Burns's knowledge of the practice of sabbats extended much beyond that of the folklore traditions. He makes the ritual seem infinitely more ridiculous than horrific, despite the list of gruesome features displayed on the old altar. Sabbats were rituals of deliberate obscenity and of desecration and included a complete inversion of Christian rites, but Burns gives us a

Devil in the shape of a dog who plays the bagpipes to provide music for his devotees to dance to. He admits that these creatures appear to have the powers to hurt, specifically referring to Nannie's capabilities in this respect, e.g.:

> For mony a beast to dead she shot,
> And perished mony a bonnie boat,
> And shook baith meikle corn and bear,
> And held the countryside in fear.

But he makes them nevertheless figures of fun. Their dances are not orgiastic nor do they lead to sacrifice and homage, but they are 'hornpipes, jigs, strathspeys and reels', exactly the kind of dances the farming community would have employed for their own enjoyment. It is doubtful that the information which would have emerged from the earlier witch trials would have been widely disseminated amongst the rural communities and in any case, it suited Burns's purpose to use the folkloric version of a particularly nasty rite and to imbue his lines with humour.

Burns may have suffered from depression or recurrent bouts of melancholia. This may have been reactive to the failures of his farming activities or to the essentially hard nature of the lifestyle of the lowland farmer. But much of his work is suffused with humour, sometimes ribald but never coarse, often displaying a mocking quality which he extended to himself as well as the other subjects of his verse. Humour has the potential to be a great defence against a depressive reaction to adversity and in the reduction of fear and of anxiety. It was probably a personal characteristic of the poet himself that caused him to write of Tam that he rode '... crooning o'er an auld Scots sonnet.' He was singing to keep up his spirits, while, as Burns admits of his own behaviour, keeping a wary eye open for bogles who might just be waiting in ambush.

Robertson in his notes to the 'Address to the Devil' says:

> That Burns believed in a personal devil may well be doubted. The humorous satire of the piece is at the

expense of popular Scottish Calvinism. The tenderness is for an imaginary being, supposed for the moment to be real, who is suffering the pains of eternal misery. The piece is anti-Calvinistic.

Carlyle in his *Essay on Burns* was of the opinion that the piece did not hang together. He thought that the gap between the events at the ale house and the *danse macabre* at Alloway old kirk was never properly bridged and so in his estimation the tragedy of Tam's adventure became a 'mere drunken phantasmagoria' and degenerated into farce.

Carlyle may have been right, in any case he was entitled to his opinion, but the survival rate and popularity of this 'farce' of 'Tam o'Shanter' has far outdistanced that of the work of Burns's near contemporaries. Whatever the gap between the realism of the alehouse and the sabbat at Alloway kirk, however folk-based Burns's concept of such a rite may have been, one can only be thankful that a childhood devoted to reading when not working and being the possessor of a very retentive memory for the tales of an old woman came to fruition in the tale of Tam as the consequence of a request from an antiquarian!

# CHRONOLOGY

1748.  William Burns leaves Clochnahill, Kincardineshire.
1749.  He is employed in the work of laying out the Meadows, Edinburgh.
1750.  He becomes gardener to the Laird of Fairly in Dundonald parish, Ayrshire.
1752.  He becomes gardener to Mr Crawford of Doonside in the same county.
1757.  He settled in a croft of seven acres in Alloway parish and married Agnes Brown of Maybole in December.
1759.  Robert was born at Alloway near Ayr on the 25th January.
1760.  Gilbert was born.
1762.  Robert's eldest sister Agnes was born.
1764.  Annabella was born.
1766.  The family moved to Mount Oliphant in May, contact was made with Betty Davidson. (Gilbert later recorded 'the soil at Mount Oliphant was almost the Poorest that he ever knew of in a state of cultivation'.)
1767.  John Murdoch was engaged as teacher on Whit Sunday, but his connection with Alloway ceased probably in November. William was born.
1769.  John was born.
1771.  Robert's youngest sister Isabella was born.
1772.  Robert went to Dalrymple parish school during the summer.
1773.  For about three weeks Robert boarded with John Murdoch who was now the Rector of Ayr academy where he studied English grammar, French and composed his first song, 'Handsome Nell'.

1774. Robert was now the main labourer on his father's farm.

1775. For a few months Robert learned land surveying at Kirkeswold and took dancing lessons against his father's wishes.

1777. The family moved on Whitsunday to a farm at Lochlie in Tarbolton.

1780. Robert starts a social club at Tarbolton.

1781. Alison Begbie rejects his proposal of marriage; he joins a masonic lodge in July and then goes to work as a flax dresser at Irvine.

1782. In January he comes home from Irvine to work on the farm at Lochlea, he is also busy writing.

1784. Burns's father aged 62 dies at Mossgiel near Mauchline. Robert begins his satirical attacks on clerical hypocrisy. On Whitsunday the family move from Lochlea to Mossgiel, a farm of some 120 acres.

1785. Robert meets Jean Armour, the daughter of a master mason of Mauchline. This was a year of great literary activity e.g. 'Halloween', 'The Cotter's Saturday Night', 'The Jolly Beggars' etc.

1786. Robert's wooing of Jean was rejected by the Armour family in the spring, there then occurred the episode of Mary Campbell. The first edition of his poems was published at Kilmarnock on 31st July. Robert decides to go to Jamaica but Dr Blacklock's letter of invitation and advice causes him to go to Edinburgh on 28th November. The poems are reviewed by Henry MacKenzie in *The Lounger* on 9th December and Robert is received into the world of rank and fashion. This was also a very productive year e.g. 'The Twa Dogs', 'The Holy Fair', 'The Brigs of Ayr' etc.

1787. A friendship developed with Mrs M'Lehose – 'Clarinda'. Robert met Dr Gregory and a post in the Excise was mooted.

1788. Robert marries Jean Armour in May and acquires a lease on a farm at Ellisland in Dumfries. After his marriage is confirmed by the Mauchline Church in

August he sets out to establish a home for his wife and child.

1789. This is the year he met Francis Grose, he also takes up his appointment as an excise man.

1790. 'Tam o'Shanter' is written.

1791. Robert leaves Ellisland at Martinmas and settles as an excise man in Dumfries in the second storey of a house in Bank Street (Wee Vennel) His salary of £50–£70 p.a. was his sole source of income.

1792. He contributed to a collection of *Original Scottish Airs* published by George Thomson. Burns's widely expressed sympathy with the revolution in France triggered an investigation into his political conduct by the Board of Excise and damaged his promotion prospects.

1793. Saw the publication of the second edition of *The Poems* in two volumes in Edinburgh in February. In May he left the Wee Vennel for a self-contained house in the Mill Vennel (Burns Street).

1794. A new and larger edition of the poems was published.

1795. Continued working for the Excise.

1796. Became ill and for some reason tried sea bathing at Brow on Solway in July, but returned home so weak on the 18th that he was scarcely able to stand. Burns died at Dumfries on Thursday 21st of rheumatic fever. He was buried at midday on Monday 25th in St Michael's churchyard. Jean survived her husband by thirty eight years.

# GLOSSARY AND NOTES

| | |
|---|---|
| Aft yont | often beyond. |
| Aiblins | perhaps, possibly. |
| Aith | oath. |
| At mony a house | this phrase refers to the fact that there was an epidemic of fever raging in the county at the time of the poet's encounter with Death. |
| Ava | of all. |
| Ayont | beyond. |
| | |
| Batts | colic. |
| Bear | barley. |
| Bicker | a short run or a wooden bowl for liquor. |
| Billie | comrade, fellow, young man. |
| Bizz | bustling, in haste. |
| Blate | bashful, sheepish. |
| Blellum | a loudmouthed fellow. |
| Blethering | talking nonsense. |
| Boddle | a small copper coin. 2p Scots. |
| Bogles | hobgoblins. |
| Bonnie yard | a beautiful place, a garden. |
| Boord | board. |
| Boortrees | elder trees or bushes. |
| Breeks | trousers. |
| Brogue | a trick. |
| Brunstane | brimstone (literally burnt stone). |
| Buchan | Dr Buchan the author of *Domestic Medicine*. |
| Bummin | humming. |

| | |
|---|---|
| Burdies | small birds; young women. |
| Byke | hive, or usually a wild bees' nest. |
| Calf ward | fine pasture. |
| Cantrip | charm, spell, trick. |
| Carlin | old woman. |
| Cassilis Downans | according to Burns, 'certain little, romantic, rocky, green hills in The neighbourhood of the abcient seat of the Earls of Cassilis.' Cassilis is near the village of Dalrymple. |
| Cauk a keel | red chalk, literally to paint and draw. |
| Cavern | the place of torment. Hell. |
| Chapmen | pedlars. |
| Cheeks o' branks | a kind of wooden curb or bridle. |
| Clachan | village. |
| Cleekit | hooked. |
| Clootie | The Devil, having hoofs. |
| Coft | bought. |
| Colean | Colzean House or castle, one of the seats of the Lords of Cassilis on the southern shore of Ayrshire. |
| Coof | simpleton. |
| Coost | cost. |
| Cootie | a kind of large spoon, the coot is the ankle. |
| Countra | country. |
| Cour | stoop. |
| Cowpit | overturned. |
| Creeshie flannen | greasy flannel. |
| Crouse | brisk, bold. |
| Crummock | a staff. |
| Cumnock hills | S.E. of Tarbolton. |
| Curmurring | rumbling. |
| Cutty sark | short shirt. |
| Dawkit twal pint hawkie | a pet cow with a white face which will give twelve pints of milk. |

| | |
|---|---|
| Ding | strike. |
| Dirl | play. |
| Douce | sober, sedate. |
| Drouthy | thirsty. |
| Duddies | rags. |
| | |
| Eldritch | wild, unearthly, hideous. |
| Ettle | to try. |
| | |
| Fairin' | a gift or a due. |
| Fechtin' | fighting. |
| Fient a wame | the devil a belly, having no belly. |
| Fodgel | plump. |
| Forbye | in addition. |
| Forgather | meet together. |
| Free the ditches | keep from falling into the ditches. |
| Fyke | trouble, fuss, bother. |
| | |
| Gab | mouth. |
| Gauger | an apprentice exciseman. |
| Gate | road. |
| Gibbet airns | chains put round a man to be hanged. |
| Gimmer | a two-year old ewe. |
| Glow'red | glared. |
| Gowans | the common daisy. |
| Grained | groaned. |
| Gree't | agreed to it. |
| Guidman | honest fellow. |
| Gully | large knife. |
| | |
| Hangie | hangman, another name given to the Devil. |
| Hornbook | schoolbook in horn covers. |
| Howlets | owls. |
| Howket dead | disinterring the deceased. |
| Hurdies | hips. |
| | |
| Ilka bore | each hole. |
| Ingle | a large fireplace. |

| | |
|---|---|
| Jinkin' | dallying. |
| Johnnie Ged's hole | an open grave. Ged was the name of the gravedigger. |
| | |
| Kail-blade/runt | cabbage leaf/stalk. |
| Kenned | known slightly. |
| Keystane | key stone, arch stone. |
| Kingshead | the second stomach of a ruminant animal. |
| Kirn | churn. |
| Kirkton Jean | Jean Kennedy, kept an inn with her sister Anne at Kirkoswald known as 'The Leddies'. |
| Kittle | excite or stir up. |
| | |
| Lag | slow. |
| Lang syne | long ago. |
| Lallan | Lowland. |
| Linket | arm in arm. |
| Linkin' | tripping. |
| Loof | palm of the hand. |
| Lough | loch. |
| Lowin' heughs | blazing pits. |
| Lowsed | loosed. |
| | |
| Mae | more. |
| Maist | most. |
| Maun | must. |
| Mawing | mowing. |
| Melder | the quantity of corn milled at one session. |
| Men | mend. |
| Misleard | unmannerly, rude. |
| Mony | many. |
| | |
| Nae mair | no more, none. |
| Naig was ca'd a shoe on | every horse that required shoeing. |
| Nappy | strong ale. |
| Near-hand | nearly, almost. |

| | |
|---|---|
| Neist | next. |
| Nick | notch. |
| Nieves | fists. |
| | |
| Out owre | out over. |
| | |
| Paisley harn | coarse linen. |
| Plew | plough. |
| Prent it | print it. |
| | |
| Ragweed | ragwort. |
| Rair | roar. |
| Rantin' | ranting. |
| Rash-bush | rushes. |
| Reamed | foamed. |
| Reekit | smoked. |
| Reestit gizz | smoke blackened face. |
| Rigwoodie hags | gallows-worthy old women. |
| | |
| Sair | sore. |
| Sark | shirt. |
| Sawin' | sowing. |
| Scar' | scare. |
| Scaud | scald. |
| Scawl | scold. |
| Scaur | a cliff or to be easily scared. |
| Sheugh | ditch or trench. |
| Shog | shake or jog. |
| Shouther | shoulder. |
| Sicker | sure. |
| Skaith | injure, hurt. |
| Skellum | numbskull. |
| Skelp/skelpit | slap or move quickly. |
| Skirl | scream, shriek. |
| Sklentin' | slanting. |
| Slade | slid. |
| Slaps | gaps or breaches in hedges and walls. |
| Smoored | smothered. |

| | |
|---|---|
| Snick-drawing dog | being crafty. |
| Souter | cobbler. |
| Spairges | scatters. |
| Spean | wean. |
| Spleuchan | tobacco pouch. |
| Spunkie | Will o' the Wisp. |
| Squattered | fluttering noise in water. |
| Stachered | staggered. |
| Stour | dust, confusion. |
| Strae-death | dying at home on the straw mattress. |
| Sugh | sigh as of wind in trees. |
| Swatch | specimen. |
| Swats | new ale. |
| Swither | hesitation. |
| | |
| Tent | attend to. |
| Thowes | thaws. |
| Tints | loses. |
| Tipenny | ale costing twopence. |
| Tirlin' the kirks | stripping the lead from church roofs. |
| Three-toed leister | trident, spear with three prongs usually for fishing. |
| Towzie tyke | shaggy dog. |
| Twal | twelve. |
| | |
| Usquabae | whisky. |
| | |
| Vauntie | proud, vain, boastful, joyous. |
| | |
| Wabster | weaver. |
| Wad | would. |
| Wark-lume | work-loom. |
| Whaur ye gaun | where are you going? |
| Whid | lie. |
| Whittle | knife. |
| Whyles | at times; now and again. |
| Winnock bunker | window seat. |
| Winsome wench and waulie | a big beautiful woman. |

| Yellow treasure | butter. |
| Yell | giving no milk. |
| Yill | ale. |

# REFERENCES

Beeching, H. C. (Ed). 1904. *The Poetical Works of John Milton.* Humphrey Mitford (Oxford University Press, London)

*Brewer's Twentieth Century Phrase and Fable* (1991, Cassell Publishers Ltd, London)

Briggs, Kathleen. *A Dictionary of Fairies* (1977, Penguin Books, Harmondsworth)

Dixon, W. M. & Grierson, H. J. C. *The English Parnassus* (1909, Clarendon Press, Oxford)

Drinkwater, J. *The Outline of Literature* (1933, George Newnes Ltd, London)

Kramer, H. & Sprenger, J. *Malleus Maleficarum.* (Translated from the Latin by Montague Summers.) (1971, Arrow Books, London)

Lindsay, M. *The Burns Encyclopaedia* (1959, Hutchinson & Co. (Publishers) Ltd, London)

Rhys, E. (Ed). *The Golden Treasury of Longer Poems* (1921, J. M. Dent, London)

Robbins, R. H. *The Encyclopaedia of Witchcraft and Demonology.* 3rd Imp. (1964, Peter Neville Ltd, London)

Robertson, J. L. *Burns Selected Poems* (1904, Clarendon Press, Oxford)

*Robert Burns Poetical Works*; Burns Centenary (Warne and Co., London)